DARE

TO

EMBRACE

NO

Activate Neuroplasticity, Empower Your Choices, Command Self-Respect, Harness The Power Of NO

SEKHAR KUMAR DEY

Copyright

Copyright © 2024 by Sekhar Kumar Dey

I dedicate this book.

To,

Mrs. Sumitra Das Biswas

My beloved mother-in-law's unwavering love and profound understanding have shaped my journey. Despite my failures in our relationship, your endless affection and trust exemplify the essence of human connection. This book, a tribute to the invaluable lessons learned from our bond, is dedicated to you. It highlights the importance of boundaries and the strength of 'no' And is a reflection of my struggle to assertively say 'no' and the transformation it brought to my life. Thank you for your enduring support, inspiring me to share my truth and nurture meaningful relationships.

My deepest gratitude,

-Sekhar Kumar Dey

How this book can help you?

"The most important thing in life is to stop saying 'I wish' and start saying 'I will."
— **David M. Schwartz**

Dare to Embrace No empowers you to reclaim control over your life in a world that demands your time and energy. This transformative guide teaches you the art of assertively saying " no, " helping you set healthy boundaries and protect your mental well-being. You'll build resilience, boost your self-esteem, and achieve a fulfilling work-life balance through practical strategies backed by sound research and real-life stories. Embrace the freedom from prioritizing your needs and values, and discover how saying "no" can lead to a happier, more authentic life. Your journey to empowerment starts here!

10 Crucial Questions in Life:

1. How can I confidently say "no" without feeling guilty or losing relationships?

2. What strategies can I use to set and maintain healthy boundaries in my life?

3. How can embracing "no" improve my mental health and reduce stress?

4. What tools can help me balance personal and professional responsibilities effectively?

5. How can I build resilience to overcome challenges and setbacks?

6. How does understanding brain science empower me to make better life decisions?

7. What are the best techniques to assertively communicate my needs and priorities?

8. How can I protect my time and energy while staying true to my goals?

9. How can I distinguish between healthy and unhealthy boundaries, and why does it matter?

10. How can improving my self-esteem enhance my personal and professional success?

Chapter 1: The Power of Childhood Resilience

In Chapter 1, readers will uncover how childhood experiences, even those marked by mischief or unconventional behavior, lay the foundation for resilience and adaptability. By reflecting on these formative years, readers will recognize the importance of embracing life's lessons and how they shape their capacity to navigate challenges.

Key benefits include understanding how peer influence can bolster or undermine your resilience. Readers will gain insights into surrounding themselves with supportive people who encourage growth. The chapter also emphasizes the value of emotional expression and vulnerability, showing how these elements are crucial for personal growth and stronger relationships.

Practical Tools:

- Resilience-building exercises that help you bounce back from setbacks.
- Peer influence assessment to ensure your social circle supports your growth.
- Emotional journaling techniques to deepen self-awareness and foster emotional expression.

Chapter 2: The Neuroscience Behind Saying No

Chapter 2 examines the brain's response to "no," revealing the profound impact this simple word has on our emotions, behavior, and decision-making. Understanding the neuroscience behind saying "no" equips readers with the knowledge to make more intentional choices that align with their values.

This chapter introduces the concept of neuroplasticity, empowering readers to take control of their mental health by engaging in practices that promote brain growth, such as mindfulness, learning, and exercise. Readers will also learn how saying "no" can reduce stress, enhance focus, and improve overall well-being.

Practical Tools:

- Neuroscience insights to enhance focus and decision-making.
- Mindfulness practices that support mental health and neuroplasticity.
- Stress-reduction techniques linked to the power of "no."

Chapter 3: Practical Strategies for Saying No

Chapter 3 provides readers with practical strategies for confidently saying "no" in both personal and professional settings. The chapter introduces the Sandwich Method, a powerful technique for delivering feedback in a way that maintains positive relationships.

Readers will learn the art of assertiveness, enabling them to express their needs and boundaries without feeling guilty. By practicing role-playing scenarios, they'll build confidence in their communication skills, making it easier to say "no" when necessary. The chapter also highlights the importance of cultural awareness, ensuring readers can navigate diverse environments effectively.

Practical Tools:

- The Sandwich Method for delivering complex messages constructively.
- Assertiveness training exercises to bolster confidence and clarity in communication.
- Role-playing scenarios to practice saying "no" in various contexts.

Chapter 4: The Power of Boundaries

In Chapter 4, readers will explore the transformative power of setting and maintaining healthy boundaries. This chapter emphasizes the importance of boundaries in protecting emotional and mental well-being. Understanding the difference between healthy and unhealthy boundaries will give readers the clarity to protect their personal space and prioritize their needs.

The chapter offers actionable strategies for establishing boundaries, such as identifying and communicating non-negotiable needs. Readers will also learn how to recognize and respond to boundary violations, ensuring respectful and supportive relationships.

Practical Tools:

- Boundary-setting exercises to identify and assert your limits.
- Techniques for effective communication of boundaries in relationships.

- Guidelines for recognizing and addressing boundary violations to maintain emotional safety.

Chapter 5: Assertiveness and Self-Care

Chapter 5 focuses on the critical connection between assertiveness and self-care. Readers will discover how assertive communication is essential for prioritizing their needs without guilt. The chapter offers practical advice on distinguishing between assertiveness and aggression, helping readers navigate interpersonal dynamics respectfully and confidently.

This chapter also emphasizes the importance of self-care in maintaining mental and physical health. Readers will learn how to create a personalized self-care routine that enhances their self-esteem and resilience, leading to a balanced and fulfilling life.

Practical Tools:

- Assertiveness exercises to express your needs clearly and confidently.
- Self-care planning tools to create a routine that supports mental and physical well-being.
- Techniques for balancing self-care with other responsibilities to prevent burnout.

Chapter 6: Building a Resilient Life

Chapter 6 ties everything together by focusing on building a resilient life through consistent self-care and assertive communication. Readers will learn how to identify and fulfill their needs, making decisions aligning with their values and goals.

This chapter highlights the importance of self-awareness, resilience, and continuous improvement. By embracing challenges as opportunities for growth, readers can cultivate a resilient mindset that supports their personal and professional success. The chapter also emphasizes accountability and flexibility, ensuring readers can adapt their self-care routines to life's inevitable changes.

Practical Tools:

- Resilience-building strategies to thrive in the face of adversity.
- Self-awareness exercises to align decisions with your actual values.
- Guidelines for maintaining accountability and flexibility in your self-care routine.

Conclusion

By reading **"Dare to Embrace No,"** readers will gain transformative insights and practical tools to navigate life with greater confidence, resilience, and mental clarity. Each chapter provides handholding techniques, from building resilience in childhood to understanding the neuroscience of saying "no" and setting boundaries that protect your well-being. The book empowers readers to take control of their lives, embrace "no" as a powerful tool for self-care, and create a balanced, fulfilling life in both personal and professional settings.

With these tools, readers will emerge more resilient, assertive, and mentally equipped to face the challenges of modern life, leading to improved mental health and well-being. Embracing "no" is not just about rejecting unnecessary demands; it's about affirming your worth, protecting your time, and creating a life that aligns with your deepest values.

Table of Contents

Chapter 1: Foundations of Resilience

"Out of suffering have emerged

the strongest souls;

the most massive characters

are seared with scars."

— Khalil Gibran

1.1: My Story: Weird Childhood

My childhood favorite activities included plucking mangoes from other trees and catching fish from their ponds. I also usually stole other students' tiffin boxes. My strong retaliation followed when other students refused to share.

Subsequently, people got used to my behavior. I couldn't be cowed down by anyone, even with a potent antidote from my father. I wept and shouted in pain when he was giving me daily doses with a thin piece of cane. I continued.

Most of the time, my friends were happy with my daily treatment at home. But few used to feel very upset and counsel me like my guardian. I was making a natural nut.

Many used to check my palms, face, and, at times, my back to see the traces of the tsunami, which was a daily ritual for me.

Even elders in my family used to resent me when I was dressed down. It was my daily ritual. I got accustomed.

At times, my father used to feel very upset with his VIP treatment of me. He took a lot of pains to make me understand not to be what I was. I remained unmoved. For me, a day remains incomplete without this ceremony of celebration. I call it my days. My style statement is that anybody could hear from far off, being a small village.

Many of my friends always remained eager to listen to my episodes. I used to explain with graphic detail. They felt as if they were beaten and gave responses, making different sounds and whispering in subdued voices or voices. Many devoured relishing.

I Was Ransacking the Ancestral Sweat and Love.

Most of the mango trees were planted by their fathers or grandfathers. They were planted with the dream that someday their children and grandchildren will enjoy the mangoes. They might have brought those baby plants from distant relatives or friends who had experienced the taste of those mangoes. Proper locations were chosen so that it wouldn't create any nuisance due to the falling of old leaves and dirty surroundings. Those plants may also provide shadows in the hot summer. There was no electricity in my village at that time. Provision for cool air and shade were visualized. It certainly fulfilled their dreams. Children were happy to enjoy those mangoes and used to sit below those enormous trees to cool down when they returned after the daily chores of cultivating the paddy fields. They even offered those mangoes when grown seasonally to the family deity of our temples. Our ancestral temple is about 300 hundred years old.

Usually, people from my village went to bed and got up early. During mango season, their first job was picking up the ripe mangoes that had fallen on the ground. They might have several plans with those mangoes. Some they used to carry to their relatives. But mostly, they ate. Surplus mangoes were used to prepare many homemade products, like extracting their tasty juices and drying and preserving them for the year.

But what happens if they find none?

I'm stuck in disbelief.

Look at the ripe mangoes that were about to fall.

They search all around.

Get overwhelmed.

Disappointed.

Disgusted.

Outburst of anger.

Strat grumbling.

Curse and disgruntled.

Then straight shouting, naming me.

Take a vow to teach me a lifetime lesson.

All the members would come out of their homes to find the facts.

Then, they unthinkingly rush to my house to complain to my father against me.

They would explain how his father collected the plants from his distant relative.

How the other day someone else cursed me.

It was one of the best mango trees in the region.

I was always the kingpin for anything that happened of such nature in my village.

My father would search for me, but it was untraceable.

After that, he would have left for the paddy field as his routine.

I would resurface once he left the house.

My mother, aunties, especially the eldest uncle, used to counsel me. It also became a ritual.

I would maintain studied silence and listen to their advice like a good boy.

A fixated target for all purposes, be it catching fish from another pond or plucking blackberries, cucumbers, cauliflower, or cabbage from another field.

That's a reputation I earned in my childhood.

My friends were undoubtedly disappointed with their mango's loss but could also imagine the catastrophes ahead.

Somehow, they were always sympathetic towards me.

After coming to school, all sorts of narration of their father's angst, followed by rushing to complain against me, started oozing out.

It was their main agenda for coming to school that day. Another impeccable method is to perform poorly in exams. It's a different matter that I never stood second in my school life.

They would earnestly plead with me not to repeat.

The episodes continued till I left my school and village once and for all to pursue my higher studies at Kolkata.

Ground Realities Were Different.

Many gardens had mango trees producing thousands of sweet mangoes of varieties.

We had several ponds, small and big.

We were the owner of the largest track of high-yielding crops.

We were then landlords.

On the contrary, my mother distributed countless mangoes to the beggars who visited us every day, and they were never refused. Once a year, there used to be a religious congregation in our family called "Mahotsav." Thousands of people from all walks of life used to flock for food for seven days—from beggars to District Magistrates.

We were Vaishnavites by religious faith. To commemorate the seven days of "nagar parikrama" of Lord Chaitanya Mahaprabhu, who was part of the religious renaissance in India. He was credited with embracing all segments of society, regardless of caste or religion. From Kings to subjects, all became his devotees. He preached the Krishna consciousness among people. This method is recommended in the scriptures, and it was given to us by Caitanya Mahaprabhu 500 years ago. He appeared in a town which is known as Navadvipa. West Bengal, India.

To date, I don't know why did I create such nuisances in my childhood.

Whether ashamed or proud of that pernicious deed, it has never bothered me to date. Judging me may be for others. I stand vulnerable. Judging me may be the job of others, not mine.

Never an Element of Regret or Remorse Haunts Me.

It never did in my life. I could focus on my studies, which used to remain unperturbed and sleep soundly. I used to get up by 4 a.m. every morning for pluck and pick. The till-day habit of getting up is only by 4 a.m. In my second innings, I read and write books for only one and a half hours before going for a morning walk.

My wife often advised me not to narrate such stupid childhood stories lest they influence my children. It never happened. My children are well-behaved, and credit goes to my wife.

At times, I wonder why at all I did those missives.

I committed all sorts of mischief at least once a day. But my friends had my friends suffered tremendous trauma. Their parents used to treat their recalcitrant children, scaring them about the inhuman consequences of my regular severe pain and agonies. It was an excellent magic wand for other parents to rein their children.

The exciting thing in my village, similar to all cross-sections of society, is that it highly reveres education.

I was one of the top two rankers in my school. Often, the tough competition used to be with my closest friend, Jayanta Sarkar, who prematurely died almost two decades ago out of throat cancer. I am proud of him. I dedicated my 3rd book, "Dare to Disown Your I."

All eyes of students and their parents attending the annual prize distribution ceremony used to fall upon me climbing up the rostrum as my name was announced to receive the prizes.

Academic Success is Universal.

It's transcendental over the ages and millenniums.

It will remain so as long as civilization exists. In Sanskrit, proverb it's said:

"Deśe deśe kalatrāṇi, deśe deśe ca bāndhavāḥ.
Tamas tu sarvatra durlabhaḥ, vidvāṁś ca vidito
bhavet."

Meaning:

"In every land, one can find a wife and relatives, but a learned

person (vidvān) is rare and revered everywhere."

It holds good till day.

These days, students need to learn resilience along with academic success to survive and progress in life. As global competition increases quickly, you will likely face serial failures to learn and prove yourself to sustain yourself in the job market and elsewhere.

Your academic excellence will enable you to reach out to the door. Still, in the actual arena, your resilience will call the shots for the rest of your life, personal and professional.

It would be best if you were seen.

That's what will change the game in your favor.

Your success is your responsibility only.

Own it.

1.2: Childhood Resilience and Peer-Influence

1. Resilience in Childhood

My father never gave up taming me. No father can let his children be a constant source of troublemakers everywhere, and that's what I was. Before I reached home, complaints reached.

I was the trigger for a cascading event that upset everyone except me. I was a recalcitrant and ardent non-compliant member of my family and neighborhood. But the rest of my family members and friends were not like me. They were always on the right side of the boundary.

My impulsive behaviors compelled others to respond the way they did. There was no other way anyone could have reacted differently. After all, those mango trees and ponds were their inherited ancestral properties. Indeed, they were entitled to enjoy them.

At that stage, I acted in a manner that I thought was appropriate. But every bitter consequence was never a deterrent for similar acts in the future. The saga of my foul behavior and aftermaths went unabated till I left my home for good at below seventeen years of age. Many thought someday I would be a branded criminal or mafia.

I felt no regret. People were tired of me, but not me. While they had a trying time, I continued despite getting solid thrash from my father.

But once in real life outside the home, submitting myself to the public domain was never an issue. I was utterly calm. In 1975, I was selected for one of the top commerce colleges in Kolkata, West Bengal, India- Goenka College of Commerce &

Business Administration. I became a student union leader, leading a fresh batch of students.

But professionally, I'm a graduate engineer in Electronics and Communication, which was a relatively unpopular branch in India in 1975. At that time, the Electrical, Mechanical, and Civil branches of engineering were calling the shots in India.

Ups and downs were my constant companion, but I was never overwhelmed. I must say my life was never smooth, like my friends. Places and organizations changed, but not me. While others used to sleep disturbed, I slept deep. I became more resolute.

We are Born and Die. But Life is an Infinite Game.

Worldwide, there is no best in any field, personal or professional. I performed reasonably well at every stage of my life, however insignificant it may be, and I'm satisfied.

Today, in my second inning at 66 years of age, I've learned the art and science of writing books and self-publishing them one after another. So far, I have written six books with four Amazon bestseller recognitions. Someday, I dream to be the No.1 bestseller. I'm on my journey unabetted.

How was it possible?

Failures were and are my constant companion. Yes, I love to fail fast and stand fast. With every failure, I learned a lot rather than regret. I don't believe in regret. It sucks you. It's unproductive and somewhat counterproductive. It constantly pushes you back, whereas everything in life is moving forward. Just do mid-course corrections and move.

You can never travel towards your destination in life in a straight line. It's primarily zig-zag (Fig.1) and full of turns and twists.

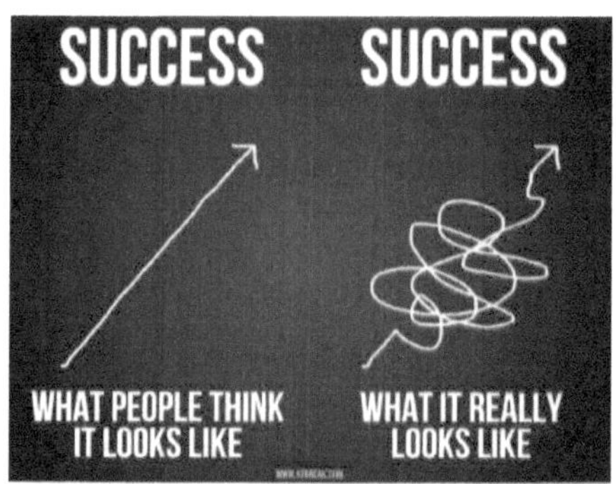

Fig.1: Picture credit: Pin it and [1]

Nothing is predictable. Nothing is absolute truth in life except death after birth. It would be best if you continued your journey. Trust the process of repeatedly failing, getting up, and marching ahead. You are bound to reach your goal. Every failure teaches you valuable life lessons, empowering you to take the next empowered step. Likewise, take one step at a time and navigate with self-confidence. You become resilient.

2. Impact of Peer Relationships

I must say, I'm blessed with a good friend circle. During my village tenure, almost everyone was my friend across all ages. I was a hero to my friends for all those mischievous activities. For them, height was how I bravely accepted my daily quota of strong medicine yet remained unchanged. Those were the moments of their jubilation as their hero used to be thrashed mercilessly yet remained unchanged.

They could have awarded me if it had been in their hands, while everyone felt extraordinary sympathy towards me. Invariably, they used to enquire about different landmarks etched all over my body. Long after that, they seriously discussed it as if I had conquered some decisive battle. I always enjoyed their reflections. Out of over-enthusiasm, they used to share my heroic acts. But often, they were reminded about the same treatment if they ever happened to be venturers like me.

Most of the time, they advised me, like my grandfather, not to repeat myself as it ended with inhuman suffering. They even tried to impress upon me the loss the owners had to bear as they expected to sell those mangoes to bear the cost of their daughter's marriage. After that, I never did any such nuisances with them.

I was generous in spending my study time at home explaining subjects like math and physics to them. They were all my neighbors. Their frequency of visiting my house increased as the examinations were drawing near. I enjoyed teaching them. Most of them rarely failed in examinations in those subjects. Maybe it was my way of giving them thanks for the tremendous love and affection they showed me.

3. Behavioral Conditioning

My father's daily punishment didn't alter my behavior. This became an accepted routine for both of us. The consequences were repetitive.

Behaviorism became a significant psychological force in the first part of the 20th century. The ideas of **John B. Watson** [2] dominated this school of thought early on. Watson focused on the principles of classical conditioning [3], once famously suggesting that he could take any person regardless of their background and train them to be anything he chose.[4]

Early behaviorists focused their interests on associative learning. **Skinner** was more interested in how the consequences of people's actions influenced their behavior.

As a behaviorist, Skinner believed examining internal thoughts and motivations to explain behavior was unnecessary. Instead, he suggested, we should examine only human behavior's external, observable causes.

Skinner used operant to refer to any *"active behavior that operates upon the environment to generate consequences."* Skinner's theory [6] explains how we acquire the range of learned behaviors we exhibit daily.[6]

1.3: Emotional Struggles and Cultural Pressures

Emotional Expression and Suppressions

Whenever I used to get thrashing, I felt pain and anger. I wept, shouting aloud so much that many used to rush to my rescue. But I never made it evident in my face before my friends. I was their hero, after all.

How can I?

Brené Brown shares in an article *A Dare to Lead + Better Up Partnership* strongly advocates you can't get courage without rumbling with vulnerability. *She says anger is the catalyst. It's an emotion that we need*

to transform into something life-giving: courage,
love, change, compassion, and justice,

Often, when we feel lost or adrift in our lives, our first instinct is to look out into the distance to find the nearest shore. But that shore, that solid ground, is within us. The anchor we are searching for is a connection, and it is internal.

Languages show us that naming an experience doesn't give the experience more power; it gives us the power of understanding and meaning.[7]

2. Cultural and Familial Expectations

Courage is an emotion that is often misunderstood. It isn't easy to define, as it is often subjective and context-dependent. There are many types of courage, each of which can be exhibited in different ways and various contexts. Some of the most influential figures in history have exhibited the courage to stand up for what is right and to challenge the status quo. In this chapter, I explore 10 of the most remarkable and courageous people in history who have changed the world.

What is Courage?

Courage is a complex emotion that can be difficult to define. 1. It is often described as the willingness to defend what is right and confront fear and adversity.

2. It faces danger, pain, or uncertainty without giving in to fear or despair.

3. It is the ability to take risks and to stand up for one's beliefs and values, even in the face of opposition or difficulty.

4. At its core, courage is the strength to take risks and act despite fear.

5. It is about having the resolve to do what is right, even when difficult.

6. Courage is not the absence of fear but rather the ability to confront and take action despite it.

7. Courage can take many forms, from physical bravery to the moral courage to speak out against injustice.

8. It can be exhibited in the face of danger or adversity or a quiet and steady determination to do what is right.

Yet the list can be longer. Here is a glimpse of your understanding.

What Makes a Person Courageous?

Courage is not a trait that everyone possesses. It requires a particular strength and determination to confront fear and take risks. Several qualities or traits can make a person more likely to exhibit courage.

Resilience: Courageous people can cope with difficult situations and setbacks without giving up. They can keep going despite the odds and focus on the end goal.

A sense of purpose: Courageous people have a strong sense of what is right and wrong and act on their beliefs. They are willing to take risks and stand up for their beliefs, even in the face of opposition.

Willingness to take risks: Courageous people are not afraid to take risks and try new things. They are willing to step outside of their comfort zone and try something that may be difficult or uncomfortable.

Moral solid compass: Courageous people are driven by a strong sense of morality and justice. They are not afraid to speak out against injustice or to take a stand, even when it is unpopular.

Self-confidence: Courageous people have faith in their abilities and their own decisions. They are not afraid to take risks and stand up for their beliefs. These people have stood up for what is right and taken risks to challenge the status quo and bring positive change.

Joan of Arc was one of the most courageous people in history. She defied the odds and led the French army to victory against the English. Her actions saved France from being conquered, and she eventually received national recognition and was canonized as a saint. Joan of Arc was fearless and never backed down from a challenge. She could face her fears and stand up to the English even when it seemed impossible. Her courage inspired others, and she is now considered one of the most influential figures in French history. Her story is a testament to the power of courage, and it's something that everyone should learn from.[8]

3. Coping Mechanism

The story of plagiarism and fraud accusations surrounding a short story written by **Helen Keller.**

Written by **Jen Hale** and **Susana Coit** in *Perkins School for the Blind*

Helen Keller was accused of ***plagiarism***, **Anne Sullivan** was accused of being a fraud, and a controversy and "trial" that would make national headlines, end the relationship Keller and Sullivan had with **Anagnos**, and end **Keller's** time at the school as a student. Keller's relationship with the school did not end permanently, however.

It starts with an event in the fall of 1891; eleven-year-old Helen Keller wrote a short story called "The Frost King" as a birthday present for Michael Anagnos, the Director of Perkins at the time. In a letter from Keller dated November 4, 1891, she introduced the gift to Anagnos with wishes for a Happy Birthday from herself, "mother and father," and "teacher" (Anne Sullivan) (Keller, "Letter to Mr. Anagnos"). In the story, King Frost and his fairies provide an origin story for the changing colors of fall leaves. Anagnos was so impressed by the story that he published it in the Perkins alum newsletter.[9]

Emad B. Algorani of Yarkmouk University and Vikas Gupta of the ***South Carolina Dept of Mental Health*** define *coping as the thoughts and behaviors mobilized to manage internal and external stressful situations.[10] It is a term used distinctively for conscious and voluntary mobilization of acts. It differs from 'defense mechanisms' that are subconscious or unconscious adaptive responses that aim to reduce or tolerate stress.[11]*

When individuals are subjected to a stressor, the varying ways of dealing with it are termed 'coping styles,' a set of relatively stable traits that determine the individual's behavior in response to stress. These are consistent over time and across situations.[12] de Boer SF, Buwalda B, Koolhaas JM.

Untangling the neurobiology of rodent coping styles: Towards neural mechanisms underlying individual differences in disease susceptibility.

Generally, coping is divided into reactive coping (a reaction following the stressor) and proactive coping (aiming to neutralize future stressors). Proactive individuals excel in stable environments because they are more routinized, rigid, and less reactive to stressors, while reactive individuals perform better in a more variable environment.[13]

Coping scales measure the type of coping mechanism a person exhibits. The most commonly used scales are COPE (Coping Orientation to Problems Experienced), Ways of Coping Questionnaire, Coping Strategies Questionnaire, Coping Inventory for Stressful Situations, Religious-COPE, and Coping Response Inventory.[14]

Coping is generally categorized into four major categories, which are [15]

1. Problem-focused, which addresses the problem causing the distress: Examples of this style include active coping, planning, restraint coping, and suppression of competing activities.

2. Emotion-focused, which aims to reduce the negative emotions associated with the problem: Examples of this style include positive reframing, acceptance, turning to religion, and humor.

3. Meaning-focused, in which an individual uses cognitive strategies to derive and manage the meaning of the situation

4. Social coping (support-seeking) involves reducing stress by seeking emotional or instrumental support from their community.

Many of the coping mechanisms prove helpful in certain situations. Some studies suggest that a problem-focused approach can be the most beneficial; other studies have consistent data that some coping mechanisms are associated with worse outcomes.[16] Stoeber J, Janssen DP. Perfectionism and coping with daily failures: positive reframing helps achieve satisfaction at the end of the day.[17]

Maladaptive coping refers to coping mechanisms that are associated with poor mental health outcomes and higher levels of psychopathology symptoms. These include disengagement, avoidance, and emotional suppression.[18] Compas BE, Jaser SS, Bettis AH, Watson KH, Gruhn MA, Dunbar JP, Williams E, Thigpen JC. Coping, emotion regulation, and psychopathology in childhood and adolescence: A meta-analysis and narrative review.

The physiology behind different coping styles is related to the serotonergic and dopaminergic input of the medial prefrontal cortex and the nucleus accumbens.[19]

The neuropeptides vasopressin and oxytocin also have essential implications relative to coping styles. On the other hand, neuroendocrinology involving the activity level of the hypothalamic-pituitary-adrenocortical axis, corticosteroids, and plasma catecholamines were unlikely to have a direct causal relationship with an individual's coping style.[20]

1.4: Moral Lessons and Social Connections

1. Role of Storytelling

Everyone has a story to share.

As humans, we like to know we're not alone, and witnessing the struggle of others reminds us of this. But many folks have a hard time tolerating unhappy endings, which is why so many movies show people conquering adversity and triumphing over tragedy. These make for a happy viewing experience but aren't always realistic. Sometimes, our stories turn negative, and we don't think we'll come out the other side. Great stories help us see that pain is inevitable and that healing and hope are possible, even when a Hollywood ending doesn't exist.

Often used in therapy, storytelling allows people to feel heard and validated, reducing anxiety, normalizing an experience, and helping people accurately perceive their experiences. Meanwhile, other people's stories can elicit empathy, help people see the world from a new perspective, provide hope, and reassure people that they're not alone in their struggles.

Some cultures discourage discussing these topics, believing that problems should be addressed only privately to avoid shame on the family or adhere to cultural norms related to self-sufficiency or emotional regulation. Such cultural norms, typically stem from various historical, environmental, and other factors, are neither good nor bad. You may feel at odds with a belief you've been raised with, and as a result, you may actively choose to reject a cultural practice that doesn't serve you. This can be a liberating or detrimental process, particularly if you don't have support when choosing a new path.

If you're considering sharing your story, and you're uncomfortable doing so, then –

1. An excellent first step is to identify people in your life who might be comfortable talking about mental health. It can also be helpful to test things out—sharing just a tiny bit of a story—before going into detail.

2. It's often wise to check in with the people you plan to talk to get their buy-in and permit them to back away if needed.

3. Sometimes, hearing the stories of others can be triggering or overwhelming and create more distance in a relationship. Ensuring the person you want to talk with is comfortable and clear about boundaries is integral to determining what and with whom to share.[21]

2. Moral Development

Ethics is the moral code that guides a person's choices and behaviors throughout life. A moral code extends beyond the individual to include what is deemed correct and wrong for a community or society.

Ethics concerns rights, responsibilities, use of language, what it means to live an ethical life, and how people make moral decisions. We may think of moralizing as an intellectual exercise, but more frequently, it attempts to make sense of our gut instincts and reactions. It's a subjective concept, and many people have strong and stubborn beliefs about what's right and wrong that can place them in direct contrast to the moral beliefs of others. Yet even though morals may vary from person to person, religion to religion, and culture to culture, many are universal, stemming from basic human emotions.[22]

The Science of Being Virtuous

Those considered morally good are considered virtuous, holding themselves to high ethical standards, while those viewed as morally wrong are considered wicked, sinful, or criminal. Morality was a key concern of **Aristotle**, who first studied questions such as ***"What is moral responsibility?" and "What does it take for a human being to be virtuous?"***

Are People Born with Morals and Ethics?

We used to think that people are born with a blank slate, but research has shown that people have an innate sense of morality [23]. Of course, parents and the greater society can certainly nurture and develop morality and ethics in children.

Can you have Morals Without Religion?

Humans are ethical and moral regardless of religion and God. People are not fundamentally good or evil. However, a Pew study found that atheists are much less likely than theists to believe that there are "absolute standards of right and wrong." In effect, atheism does not undermine morality, but the atheist's conception of morality [23] may depart from that of the traditional theist.

Do Animals Have Morals?

Animals are like humans—and humans are animals, after all. Many studies have been conducted across animal species, and more than 90 percent of their behavior can be identified as "prosocial" or positive. Plus, you won't find mass warfare in animals like humans. Hence, in a way, you can say that animals are [24] more moral than humans.

What is the Difference Between Moral Psychology and Moral Philosophy?

The examination of moral psychology [25] involves the study of moral philosophy. Still, the field is more concerned with how a person comes to make a right or wrong decision rather than what decisions they should have made. Character, reasoning, responsibility, and altruism, among other areas, also come into play, as does the development of morality.

Understanding Amorality

The seven deadly sins, first enumerated in the sixth century by Pope Gregory I, represent the sweep of immoral behavior. Also known as the cardinal sins or seven deadly vices are vanity, jealousy, anger, laziness, greed, gluttony, and lust. People who demonstrate these immoral behaviors are often considered flawed. Some modern thinkers suggest that virtue often disguises a hidden vice, depending on where we tip the scale [26].

What is the Difference Between Being amoral and Being Immoral?

An amoral person has no sense of, or care for, what is right or wrong. There is no regard for either morality or immorality. Conversely, an immoral person knows the difference but does the wrong thing regardless. The amoral politician, for example, has no conscience and makes choices based on his own needs; he is oblivious to whether his actions are right or wrong.

What is Amoral Behavior?

One could argue that Wells Fargo's actions, for example, were amoral if the bank had no sense of right or wrong. In the 2016 fraud scandal, the bank created fraudulent savings and checking accounts for millions of clients, unbeknownst to them. Of course, if the bank knew what it was doing all along, the scandal would be labeled immoral.

Why do Some People Lie a Lot?

Everyone tells white lies to a degree, and often, the lie is done for the greater good. However, the idea that a small percentage of people tell the lion's share of lies [27] is the **Parcto principle**, the law of the vital few. *It is 20 percent of the population that accounts for 80 percent of a behavior.*

Do People Know What's Right from Wrong?

We do know what is right from wrong [28]. If you harm and injure another person, that is wrong. However, what is suitable for one person may be wrong for another. An excellent example of this dichotomy is *the religious conservative who thinks that a woman's right to her body is morally wrong. In this case, one's ethics are based on one's values, and the moral divide between values can be vast.*

The Stages of Moral Development

Psychologist Lawrence Kohlberg established his stages of moral development in 1958. This framework has led to current research into moral psychology. Kohlberg's work addresses how we think of right and wrong and is based on Jean Piaget's theory of moral judgment for children. His stages include pre-conventional, *conventional, and post-conventional, and what we learn in one stage is integrated into the subsequent stages.*

What is the Pre-Conventional Stage?

The pre-conventional stage is driven by obedience and punishment [29]. This is a child's view of what is right or wrong. Examples of this thinking are: *"I hit my brother, and I received a time-out." "How can I avoid punishment?" "What's in it for me?"*

What is the Conventional Stage?

The conventional stage is when we accept societal views on rights and wrongs. *In this stage, people follow the rules with a good boy and a lovely girl orientation. An example of this thinking is "Do it for me."* This stage also includes law-and-order morality: *"Do your duty."*

What is the Post-Conventional Stage?

The post-conventional stage is more abstract: *"Your right and wrong is not my right and wrong."* This stage goes beyond social norms, and an individual develops his moral compass, sticking to personal principles of what is ethical.[30]

3. Social Dynamics in Small Communities

Social Visibility and Knowledge

The social dynamics of life in a small community impact people's life, their problems, and their understanding of their difficulties [31

In small communities, people live nearby and witness everyday happenings. They know each other intimately, which helps them behave in a particular manner, maintain social harmony, and avoid conflicts.

Anthony P. Cohen, a ***social anthropologist*** known for his work on communities, points out that if social order and stability are to be preserved, individuals must, through various mechanisms, 'somehow subordinate individuality to commonality' (1982, p 11) [32]. He noted, *"Even in the closest social association, relations of inferiority and superiority are* *rarely expressed, although they may well be tacitly recognized"* (1982, p 11).

Cooperation and Social Norms

Small communities have a few people living together. In my village, approximately 1000 people resided in 1975. The community members used to coordinate any event, like playing games, organizing wedding ceremonies, festivals, medical care, or cremation. These unwritten norms and practices helped resolve conflicts and disputes and promote harmonious living. Supporting each other was the way of life.

Besides providing a convenient framework to address the evolution of moral systems, indirect reciprocity offers a simple and plausible explanation for the prevalence of cooperation among unrelated individuals. *Helping someone may increase an individual's reputation, which may change the predisposition of others to help them.* This, however, depends on what is reckoned as a good or bad action, i.e., on the adopted social norm responsible for raising or damaging a reputation. *In particular, whether social norms can foster cooperation in small-scale societies while enduring the vast plethora of stochastic effects inherent to finite populations remains an open question.*[33]

Balancing Individuality and Community

In a close community, the approach is all for one and one for all. Individuality is overridden by community priority.

Under such circumstances, conflict is bound to exist. Often, individual aspirations and desires have little place.

Subordination is an essential component of any community. It ensures social cohesion, stability, and continuity.

Many challenges exist in small communities, such as gender roles, the importance of confidentiality, and ideas of belonging. These essential ingredients require a delicate balance between individuality and maintaining social harmony.

4. Intergenerational Impact

Intergenerational is the interaction between members of different generations [34]

In the social sciences, intergenerational transmission refers to the transfer of economic or social status across generations. These cross-generational transfers occur through various means, including the inheritance of occupational status, educational attainment, earnings, and wealth.

According to social identity theory [35], people classify themselves and others based on perceived similarities and differences. Therefore, individuals may seek to classify themselves as belonging to a particular generation because they perceive oneness with traits popularly associated with other group members and classify others into separate "out-groups" based on dissimilar characteristics. *As individuals create in and out-groups from generational identities, interactions between members can be impacted, and conflict can occur.*[36] This bias between generations occurs because of the human need to belong to a social group to provide a sense of social identity, pride, and self-esteem. Still, it may also create stereotypes about those in different social groups, including generations.[37]

Under the intergenerational contract or agreement, written and unwritten rules of the redistribution of social status, which include wealth, power, and prestige, can exist between generations.[38] It is the principle that different generations support each other across the different stages of their lives.[5] This contract functions in both our responsibilities within our families and society as a whole, as well as the role of the government. *The intergenerational contract generally works because everyone puts in and takes out.* The goal of the contract is to support the older generations because as we grow older, we will believe and expect that we will be treated the same.[39][40]

Advantages of Intergenerational Relationships

Intergenerational Impact is a powerful force, especially in modern scenarios when life is globally challenged on various socio-economic-technological fronts.

A very high degree of intolerance threatens regular dialogue among people worldwide. Disruptions in multifaceted forms are the order of the day.

Fostering connections between different age groups can certainly help build more understanding, cohesive, and resilient societies.

Let the blessings of Intergenerational bonding perpetuate with all its flaws and shortcomings to ensure:

1. Enhanced Social Cohesion

A community has different generations living together. Proper bonding among the members is imperative for promoting a stronger sense of community and belonging. Then, the accrued benefits are realized.

2. Improved Mental Health

Different engagement processes, such as attending birthdays and marriage ceremonies, providing support, etc., contribute to harnessing the combined pool of individuals in the group.

It's essential for older adults. As they age, their physical and mental inabilities increase, and the younger generation must uphold them with diverse support and make them inclusive in every activity. *A shared responsibility goes a long way to mitigate the challenging situations of older adults. If nothing is possible, give them your company in turn and thus keep them cheerful and mentally engaged.*

2. Educational Gains

I often visited my senior cousins or friends during childhood to understand some subjects. *In a community, this is one of the best advantages of getting mentors through our seniors. It certainly provided better outcomes.*

3. A Social Insurance

The most significant advantage of any community living is it acts as social insurance against sudden threatening situations or the hour of emergencies or accidents. It provides unconditional support to the initial mush needed. It's an all-weather support to each other.

Who knows who is the next?

1.5: 10 Main Takeaways

1. Childhood Mischief: Embrace the lessons from my unconventional childhood experiences, emphasizing resilience and adaptability in facing challenges.

2. Value of Resilience: Resilience is essential for overcoming adversity. My childhood mischief taught me to persist despite the consequences.

3. Peer Influence: Understand how peer relationships can shape behavior and reinforce the importance of surrounding oneself with supportive friends.

4. Emotional Expression: Acknowledge the significance of emotional expression and vulnerability as pathways to personal growth and connection.

5. Cultural Expectations: Explore how cultural and familial expectations influence behavior, highlighting the courage needed to navigate these pressures.

6. Learning from Failures: Appreciate that failures are opportunities for learning and growth, helping to develop resilience and a strong sense of self.

7. Academic Excellence: While academic success is essential, resilience is crucial for long-term personal and professional fulfillment.

8. Ethical Foundation: Understanding ethics is crucial for making moral decisions. It emphasizes the importance of a shared moral code that guides individual and community behavior.

9. Moral Development: Recognizing the stages of moral development helps us appreciate how our sense of right and wrong evolves, shaped by experiences and societal influences.

10. Intergenerational Relationships: Fostering connections between generations enhances social cohesion and promotes mutual support, contributing to mental well-being and community resilience.

Chapter 2: The Neuroscience Behind Saying NO

"Neurons that fire together wire together." —
-Donald Hebb

2.1: Brain Regions Involved

The oldest, shortest words – 'yes' and 'no' –
require the most thought."
-Pythagoras

One of the words you have heard the maximum number of times in your life is "NO" rather than "YES."

"Focusing is about saying no," says **Steve Jobs**.[41]

"I know some of you spent a lot of time working on stuff we put a bullet in the head of. I apologize. I feel your pain, but Apple suffered from lousy engineering management for several years. I must say it; people went in eighteen different directions, doing arguably interesting things in each one.

Good engineers. Lousy management. And what happened was you look at the farm that's been created with all these different animals going in different directions, and it doesn't add up. The total is less than the sum of the parts. And so we had to decide what are the fundamental directions we're going in and what makes sense and what doesn't, and there were a bunch of things that didn't, and microcosmically, they might have made sense macrocosmically, they made no sense.

And you know the most challenging thing is... when you think about focusing, right? You think that focusing well is saying yes! No. Focusing... is about saying no."

Since birth, we have learned to associate "Yes" with approvals and encouragement, whereas "No" with prohibitions and disapprovals. Therefore, we attribute emotional valence to words, and their value or reward or punishment is context-dependent and reinforced by actions and repeated situations over time. But what is happening in the brain in response to "Yes" (*positive valanced word*) or "No" (*negative valanced world*)?

The neural basis of these mechanisms has not been deeply explored so far. However, the study of Alia-Klein et al. (2007) [42] aimed to investigate the different response patterns associated with spoken Yes or No by implementing *functional Magnetic Resonance Imaging* (fMRI) in a group of healthy volunteers.

Based on previous research, this fMRI study *hypothesized that the words "No" (negative) and "Yes" (positive) would be perceived as having a different valence and, therefore, generate an opposite brain-behavior response.*

Moreover, based on a previous study, the *orbitofrontal cortex* (OFC) would respond differently and according to the specific emotional valence that is attributed to the word [43].

Hence, attending to "No" as a valanced signal would allow anger control to adapt and adjust the behaviours accordingly. However, ignoring a "No" as a prohibitive signal would prevent a behavior change. Results demonstrated that the exposition to No was perceived as negatively valenced, generating slower *response times* (RTs) and evoking a negative signal in the right OFC.

Differently, the exposition to "Yes" was perceived as positively valenced, thus leading to faster RTs and evoking a positive signal in an adjacent area of the OFC.

Furthermore, the negative valence related to "No" and the personality trait of anger control were also associated with higher activity in the OFC in response to this word. *Therefore, the authors concluded that the sensitivity to the "No" as the prohibitive command would evolve during childhood while interacting with caregivers, and where the activation of the lateral OFC would be involved as underlying neural mechanisms of emotional regulation, social and developmental processes* [44] [45].

2.2: Neuroplasticity

Let's break the word *"neuroplasticity"* down. *"Neuro"* refers to the nervous system of the brain and spinal cord, and *"plasticity"* refers to change.

Experts have yet to determine the limits of the brain's abilities. Some believe we may never fully understand them all. However, evidence does support the existence of one of its most essential processes: neuroplasticity.[46]

Can We, as Adults, Grow New Nerve Cells?

In her TED Talk, **Sandrine Thuret**, a ***neuroscientist***, shares her research findings, which provide insights on how we can help our brains perform neurogenesis better—improving mood, increasing memory formation, and preventing the decline associated with aging.

"There's still some confusion about that question, as this is a relatively new field of research. For example, I was talking to one of my colleagues, Robert, who is an oncologist, and he was telling me, "Sandrine, this is puzzling. Some of my patients who have been told they are cured of their cancer still develop symptoms of depression.

"And I responded to him, "Well, from my point of view, that makes sense. The drug you give your patients that stops the cancer cells multiplying also stops the newborn neurons generated in their brain." And then Robert looked at me like I was crazy and said, "But Sandrine, these are adult patients -- adults do not grow new nerve cells.

"And much to his surprise, I said, "Well, actually, we do." And this is a phenomenon that we call neurogenesis. [Neurogenesis] Robert is not a neuroscientist, and when he went to medical school, he was not taught what we know now -- that the adult brain can generate new nerve cells. So, Robert, you know, being the good doctor he is, wanted to come to my lab to understand the topic better.

Neurogenesis:

I took him on a tour of one of the most exciting parts of the brain regarding neurogenesis—the hippocampus. This grey structure in the brain's center has long been important for learning, memory, mood, and emotion.

However, we have learned more recently that this is one of the unique structures of the adult brain where new neurons can be generated. And if we slice through the hippocampus and zoom in, what you see here in blue is a newborn neuron in an adult mouse brain. So, when it comes to the human brain -- my colleague Jonas Frisén from the Karolinska Institute has estimated that we produce 700 new neurons per day in the hippocampus.

You might think this is not much compared to our billions of neurons. But by the time we turn 50, we will have all exchanged the neurons we were born within that structure with adult-born neurons. So why are these new neurons important, and what are their functions? First, we know that they're essential for learning and memory.

Spatial Recognition:

In the lab, we have shown that if we block the adult brain's ability to produce new neurons in the hippocampus, we block specific memory abilities. This is especially true for spatial recognition—how you navigate the city. We are still learning a lot, and neurons are essential not only for memory capacity but also for memory quality.

They will have helped add time to our memory and help differentiate similar memories, like: How do you find the bike that you park at the station every day in the same area but in a slightly different position? More interesting to my colleague

Robert is the research we have been doing on neurogenesis and depression.

Neurogenesis and Depression:

So, in an animal model of depression, we have seen that we have a lower level of neurogenesis. If we give antidepressants, then we increase the production of these newborn neurons, and we decrease the symptoms of depression, establishing a clear link between neurogenesis and depression. Moreover, if you block neurogenesis, then you block the efficacy of the antidepressant.

So, by then, Robert had understood that very likely his patients were suffering from depression even after being cured of their cancer because the cancer drug had stopped newborn neurons from being generated. And it will take time to generate new neurons that reach normal functions.

Neurogenesis is a Target of Choice:

So, collectively, we have enough evidence to say that neurogenesis is a target of choice if we want to improve memory formation or mood or even prevent the decline associated with aging or stress.

Can We Control Neurogenesis?

So, the next question is: Can we control neurogenesis? The answer is yes. We are now going to do a little quiz. I will give you a set of behaviors and activities, and you tell me if you think they will increase or decrease neurogenesis.

Are we ready?

OK, let's go.

So, what about learning?

Increasing?

Yes.

Learning will increase the production of these new neurons.

How about stress?

Yes, stress will decrease the production of new neurons in the hippocampus.

How about sleep deprivation?

Indeed, it will decrease neurogenesis.

How about sex?

Yes, it will increase the production of new neurons.

However, it's all about balance here. We don't want to fall into a situation - about too much sex leading to sleep deprivation.

How about getting older?

So, the neurogenesis rate will decrease as we get older, but it is still occurring.

And then, finally, how about running?

Judge that by yourself.

The Environment Can Have an Impact on the Production of New Neurons:

This is one of the first studies carried out by one of my mentors, Rusty Gage, from the Salk Institute, showing that the environment can impact the production of new neurons. Here, you see a section of a mouse's hippocampus with no running wheel in its cage. The little black dots are newborn neurons-to-be

And now, you see a section of the hippocampus of a mouse that had a running wheel in its cage. So, you see the massive increase of the black dots representing the new neurons-to-be. So, activity impacts neurogenesis, but that's not all.

What you Eat will Affect the Production of New Neurons in the Hippocampus:

So here we have a sample diet—of nutrients that have been shown to have efficacy: Calorie restriction of 20 to 30 percent will increase neurogenesis. Intermittent fasting—spacing the time between your meals—will increase neurogenesis. Intake of flavonoids, which are contained in dark chocolate or blueberries, will increase neurogenesis.

Omega-3 fatty acids, present in fatty fish like salmon, will increase the production of these new neurons. Conversely, a diet rich in high saturated fat will hurt neurogenesis. Ethanol -- intake of alcohol -- will decrease neurogenesis. However, not everything is lost; resveratrol, contained in red wine, has been shown to promote the survival of these new neurons.

So next time you are at a dinner party, you might want to reach for this possibly "neurogenesis-neutral" drink. Japanese groups are fascinated with food textures and have shown that a soft diet impairs neurogenesis, as opposed to food that requires mastication—chewing—or crunchy food.

So, all of this data, where we need to look at the cellular level, has been generated using animal models. However, this diet has also been given to human participants, and we can see that it modulates memory and mood in the same direction as it modulates neurogenesis. For example, calorie restriction will improve memory capacity. In contrast, a high-fat diet will exacerbate symptoms of depression—as opposed to omega-3 fatty acids, which increase neurogenesis and also help to decrease the symptoms of depression.

So, we think diet's effect on mental health, memory, and mood is mediated by the production of new neurons in the hippocampus. And it's not only what you eat but also the texture of the food, when you eat it, and how much of it you eat. On our side- neuroscientists interested in neurogenesis- we need to understand the function of these new neurons better and how we can control their survival and production." [47]

Stress Reduction:

While saying "no" can be empowering and liberating to some, it can also be intimidating or uncomfortable for others. Society sometimes teaches us that "no" is impolite and inconsiderate.

Yet there are clear benefits to the word no. Saying no can create more mental health stability by helping with self-care and building your self-esteem [48] and confidence [49] by setting boundaries. Saying no may be daunting, but there are ways to simplify the process.

Why We Say Yes?

Perhaps the best way to explore why saying no is essential is to analyze why we often say yes.

1. Avoiding Confrontation

Immensely few people enjoy confrontation. When we feel that saying no will put more pressure or tension on us, we tend to say yes to prevent those feelings.

2. Pleasing Others

Think of a "Yes Man" – someone who all too often seemingly says yes to please another person. Most of us do this to a lesser extent because people generally want to help the interests of others.

3. Fear of Missing Out (FOMO)

FOMO is very much a real thing, and when we feel as if saying no will prevent us from experiencing something we perceive others will, saying yes feels like the only natural option.

4. Compulsivity

Sometimes, people are compelled to "overdo it" and say yes to any situation.

Power of Saying No:

The power of saying no comes down to its effects on our brains. When we say no more often, we shift the way our brain thinks and reacts to situations, allowing us more ability to make decisions for ourselves. This has a tremendous effect on our mental health, as it allows us to value ourselves more.

Learn to Say No:

Even if we implement these thought processes into our mindsets, we will still find ourselves in numerous situations where saying "yes" is the better decision. So, how do we know precisely when to say no? How do we know if it feels right or wrong

When we learn to say no, we must ask ourselves specific questions about the situation: will saying yes prevent us from focusing on something more substantial? Will saying yes make me even more tired or burnt out? These questions give us the framework for when it's finally time to say no.

Other tips that are recommended to help you learn to say no include:

1. Rehearse – Ask yourself these questions, and rehearse how you wish to convey your point.

2. Be honest – There is never a need to lie about why you are saying no.

3. Offer alternatives – Sometimes, providing another way to go about something can help prevent you from saying yes.

4. Do not rush – You don't need to say no to everything, but give yourself time to think through the consequences of committing and then correctly give a response.

Your Mental Health is Key:

With more light now shed on why saying no is essential, it's time to prioritize your mental health. Setting boundaries in life can protect your mental health and provide you with ways to combat certain negatives more productively. But if you believe your mental health may need help prioritizing.[50]

Though some causes of low self-esteem can't be changed, such as genetic factors, early childhood experiences, and personality traits, you can take steps to feel more secure and valued. Remember that no one person is less worthy than the next. Keeping this in mind may help you maintain a healthy sense of self-esteem.

Self-Esteem Boost:

What is Self-Esteem?

Healthy self-esteem can influence your motivation, mental well-being, and overall quality of life. However, having self-esteem that is either too high or too low can be problematic. Better understanding your unique self-esteem level can help you strike a balance that is just right for you.[51]

Critical elements of self-esteem include:

- Self-confidence.
- Feelings of security.
- Identity

- Sense of belonging.
- Feeling of competence.

Other terms often used interchangeably with self-esteem include self-worth, self-regard, and self-respect.

Self-esteem tends to be lowest in childhood and increases during adolescence and adulthood, reaching a relatively stable and enduring level. This makes self-esteem similar to the stability of personality traits over time.[52]

How to Embrace Self-Acceptance?

Self-esteem impacts decision-making, relationships, emotional health, and overall well-being. It also influences motivation [1], as people with a healthy, optimistic view of themselves understand their potential and may feel inspired to take on new challenges.[53]

Four key characteristics of healthy self-esteem are:
1. *A firm understanding of one's skills.*
2. *The ability to maintain healthy relationships with others as a result of having a healthy relationship with oneself.*
3. *Realistic and appropriate personal expectations.*
4. *An understanding of one's needs and the ability to express those needs.*

People with low self-esteem tend to feel less sure of their abilities and may doubt their decision-making process. They may not feel motivated to try novel things because they don't believe they can reach their goals. Those with low self-esteem may have issues with relationships and expressing their needs. They may also experience low levels of confidence and feel unlovable and unworthy.

People with high self-esteem may overestimate their skills and feel entitled to succeed, even without the ability to back up their belief in themselves. They may struggle with relationship issues and block themselves from self-improvement because they are so fixated on seeing themselves as perfect [54].

Factors That Affect Self-Esteem:

Many factors can influence self-esteem. Your self-esteem may be impacted by:

- Age.
- Disability,
- Genetics,
- Illness,
- Physical abilities,
- Socioeconomic status,[55]
- Thought patterns,

Racism and discrimination have also been shown to have adverse effects on self-esteem.[56] Genetic factors that help shape a person's personality can play a role, but life experiences are considered the most critical factor.

Our experiences often form the basis for our overall self-esteem. For example, low self-esteem might be caused by overly critical or negative assessments from family and friends. Those who experience what **Carl Rogers** called unconditional positive regard [57] are likelier to have healthy self-esteem.

Healthy Self-Esteem:

There are some simple ways to tell if you have healthy self-esteem. You probably have healthy self-esteem if you:

1. Avoid dwelling on past negative experiences [58]

2. Believe you are equal to everyone else, no better and no worse

3. Express your needs

4. Feel confident

5. Have a positive outlook [59] on life

6. Say "No" [60] when you want to

7. See your overall strengths and weaknesses and accept them

Having healthy self-esteem can help motivate you to reach your goals. You can navigate life knowing that you can accomplish what you set your mind to.

Low Self-Esteem:

Low self-esteem [61] may manifest in a variety of ways. If you have low self-esteem:

1. You may believe that others are better than you.

2. You may find expressing your needs difficult.

3. You may focus on your weaknesses.

4. You may frequently experience fear, self-doubt, and worry.

5. You may have a negative outlook on life and feel a lack of control.[62]

6. You may have an intense fear of failure.

7. You may have trouble accepting positive feedback.

8. You may have trouble saying "No" and setting boundaries.

9. You may put other people's needs before your own.

10. You may struggle with confidence [63].

Low self-esteem has the potential to lead to a variety of mental health disorders, including anxiety disorders and depressive disorders. You may also find pursuing your goals and maintaining healthy relationships challenging. Having low self-esteem can seriously impact your quality of life and increase your risk of experiencing suicidal thoughts.[64]

Excessive Self-Esteem:

Overly high self-esteem is often mislabelled as narcissism [65]. However, some distinct traits [66] differentiate these terms.

Individuals with narcissistic traits may appear to have high self-esteem, but their self-esteem may be high or low and unstable, constantly shifting depending on the given situation.[67]

Those with excessive self-esteem:

1. *May be preoccupied with being perfect.*

2. *May focus on always being right.*

3. *May believe they cannot fail.*

4. *May believe they are more skilled or better than others.*

5. *May express grandiose ideas.*

6. *May grossly overestimate their skills and abilities.*

When self-esteem is too high, it can result in relationship problems, difficulty with social situations, and an inability to accept criticism.

How to Improve Self-Esteem?

Fortunately, there are steps that you can take to address problems with your perceptions of yourself and faith in your abilities. How do you build self-esteem? Some actions that you can take to help improve your self-esteem [68] include:

1. Become more aware of negative thoughts. Learn to identify the distorted thoughts [69] that are impacting your self-worth.

2. Challenge negative thinking patterns. When you engage in negative thinking, try countering those thoughts [70] with more realistic and positive ones.

3. Use positive self-talk. Practice reciting positive affirmations [71] to yourself.[72]

4. Practice self-compassion. Practice forgiving yourself [73] for past mistakes and move forward by accepting all parts of yourself.

Low self-esteem can contribute to or be a symptom of mental health disorders, including anxiety and depression. Consider speaking with a doctor or therapist about available treatment options, including psychotherapy (in-person or online), medications, or a combination.

2.4: Emotional Intelligence

What is Emotional Intelligence?

Emotional intelligence (EQ) is the ability to understand, use, and manage one's feelings to reduce stress, communicate effectively with others, empathize with them, and overcome challenges.

The term was made famous by psychologist Daniel Goleman in his book Emotional Intelligence: Why It Can Matter More Than IQ, in which he redefines what it is to be innovative. In the book, Goleman lays out five categories of emotional intelligence.

Five Components of Emotional Intelligence

Self-awareness. A person has a healthy sense of emotional intelligence and self-awareness if they understand their strengths and weaknesses and how their actions affect others. A person with emotional self-awareness is usually receptive to and able to learn from constructive criticism more than one who doesn't have emotional self-awareness.

Self-regulation. A person with high emotional intelligence can exercise restraint and control when expressing emotions.

Motivation. People with high emotional intelligence are self-motivated, resilient, and driven by an inner ambition rather than being influenced by outside forces, such as money or prestige.

Empathy. An empathetic person has compassion and can connect with other people emotionally, helping them respond genuinely to other people's concerns.

Social skills. Emotionally intelligent people can build trust with other people and can gain respect from the people they meet quickly.

What is the Difference Between IQ and EQ?

If emotional intelligence is a type of intelligence, how does it differ from the mental type? In part by how it's measured. One's intelligence quotient (IQ) is a score derived from standardized tests designed to measure intelligence. Your IQ relates directly to your intellectual abilities, like how well you learn, understand, and apply information. People with higher IQs can think abstractly and make mental connections more easily.

Emotional intelligence is very different. Sometimes called EI (for Emotional Intelligence) or EQ (for Emotional Intelligence Quotient), emotional intelligence is like using emotions to think and enhance our reasoning. Those with high emotional intelligence can manage their emotions, use their emotions to facilitate their thinking and understand the emotions of others.

Some say emotional intelligence is more beneficial for a career than IQ, although others argue IQ matters more. Emotional intelligence is essential at work, regardless of which is more important.

Importance of Emotional Intelligence:

Just because you walk through the door and into an office building does not mean you check your emotions at that door before starting work, although it used to seem that way. In reality, emotions have always been in the workplace, but they were to be kept in check, with people pretending not to feel while on the clock.

Companies hiring want to ensure they choose candidates who mesh well with existing teams. As a result, about 71 percent of organizations now value emotional intelligence in an employee over IQ. Even the most intelligent person needs good people skills to succeed these days. A high IQ alone is no longer enough.

What we perceive as reality often differs from what those around us see. Start getting input from others to understand how you come across in emotionally charged situations.

Observe. Pay more attention to your emotions once you've increased your self-awareness and understand how you're coming across.

Pause for a moment. Stop and think before you act or speak. It's hard to do, but keep working, and it will become a habit.

Become more empathetic. Try understanding the "why" behind another person's feelings or emotions.

Choose to learn from criticism. Who likes criticism? Possibly no one. But it's inevitable. We can grow in emotional intelligence by learning from criticism rather than defending our behaviors.

Practice, practice, practice. Becoming more emotionally intelligent won't happen overnight, but it can happen—with effort, patience, and much practice.[74][75]
 Mental Health. Everybody can benefit from understanding why saying no is essential to do in life. Humans are inclined to want to say yes in situations, whether to let someone down or not to let themselves down.[75]

1. Understanding Brain Responses: The brain reacts differently to "yes" and "no," with distinct regions involved in processing these words, impacting our behavior and emotions.

2. Neuroscience of Focus: Saying "no" enhances focus and decision-making, as emphasized by Steve Jobs' experiences in managing complexity.

3. Emotional Valence: "No" often carries a negative connotation, leading to slower responses and negative emotions, influencing how we interact socially.

4. Childhood Learning: Our sensitivity to "no" develops through caregiver interactions, shaping our emotional regulation and social behavior.

5. Neuroplasticity: The brain's ability to change (neuroplasticity) enables adults to grow new neurons, impacting memory, mood, and overall mental health.

6. Impact of Lifestyle: Engaging in healthy behaviors like learning and exercise can boost neurogenesis, promoting better mental health.

7. Stress Management: Saying "no" can reduce stress and enhance self-care, improving self-esteem and confidence.

8. Boundaries Matter: Establishing boundaries by saying "no" is essential for maintaining mental health and prioritizing personal needs.

9. Self-Esteem Development: Healthy self-esteem is crucial for motivation and decision-making, affecting overall quality of life.

10. Embrace Self-Acceptance: Recognizing and valuing oneself is critical to developing healthy relationships and achieving personal goals.

Chapter 3: Practical Strategies for Saying NO

"When you say yes to others, make sure you are not saying no to yourself."
- Paulo Coelho

3.1: The Sandwich Method

In my childhood, the process of feedback from my teachers used to be something like:

1. I was usually praised for my good academic performance and extracurricular activities, and I used to win several prizes for them.

2. Then straight caning by my teachers on my palm.

3. This is invariably followed by advice not to repeat stupid acts; otherwise, it's bound to hamper my performances.

It was somewhat akin to today's Sandwich method of counseling.

This technique was in vogue in almost all schools in India before the 1970s. I passed school in 1975.

This is famously known as the Sandwich Method.

What is this Sandwich method?

Simply speaking, place the bitter pill between two pieces of sweet bread.

The 'feedback sandwich' was popularized in the 1980s by **Mary Kay Ash**, the founder of *Mary Kay Cosmetics*, who advised managers to sandwich critical remarks between layers of praise.

Why is it so Popular?

A feedback sandwich is a popular tool for several reasons.

First, it can effectively balance negative feedback with positive reinforcement, which can help reduce criticism's impact and make it more digestible.

Second, it encourages the person receiving feedback to listen [76] more actively and be more open to constructive criticism [77].

Finally, it promotes a culture of support and encouragement, which can benefit individual growth and overall team morale.

How Does the Feedback Sandwich Work?

The feedback sandwich is a communication technique that provides constructive feedback in a supportive and balanced way. Its structure is simple: it begins with positive feedback, followed by constructive feedback, and ends with another round of positive feedback.

1. **Balances Negative Feedback with Positive Feedback:**

One of the main advantages of using the feedback sandwich is that it helps to balance negative feedback with positive feedback. By starting and ending the feedback conversation with positive feedback, the feedback giver can create a more supportive and non-threatening atmosphere that makes it easier for the person receiving feedback to be receptive to constructive feedback.

2. **Encourages People to Listen More:**

Another advantage of using the feedback sandwich is that it encourages people to listen more to the feedback. When people receive positive feedback at the beginning of the conversation, they are more likely to be open to the feedback that will follow. This approach helps to build trust between the feedback giver and receiver and can lead to a more productive and meaningful feedback conversation.

3. **Promotes a Constructive and Supportive Feedback Culture:**

The feedback sandwich also promotes a constructive and supportive feedback culture. When people receive balanced and supportive feedback, they are more likely to be motivated to work on the areas for improvement. This approach helps to create a culture where feedback is seen as a tool for growth and development.

4. Increases the Likelihood of Meaningful Change:

Finally, the feedback sandwich increases the likelihood of meaningful change. When people receive specific and actionable feedback, they are more likely to be able to make changes that lead to improvement. The feedback sandwich helps ensure that the feedback is given clearly and respectfully, focusing on actions and behaviors rather than the person's character or personality.

Disadvantages of the Feedback Sandwich:

While the feedback sandwich has its advantages, it's not without its criticisms and limitations. In this section, we'll explore some of the disadvantages of using the feedback sandwich:

1. Can Be Seen as Manipulative or Insincere:

One of the main criticisms of the feedback sandwich is that it can be seen as manipulative or insincere. When people receive feedback that starts and ends with positive comments, they may feel that the negative feedback is being softened or sugar-coated.

2. May Not Work in All Situations:

Another disadvantage of using the feedback sandwich is that it may not work in all situations. For example, if the feedback is about a serious or urgent issue, using the feedback sandwich may not be appropriate as it may downplay the seriousness of the situation.

3. Can Be Difficult to Deliver Effectively:

The feedback giver needs to be skilled at clearly delivering both positive and negative feedback and ensuring that the positive feedback is genuine and specific.

4. May Not Address Underlying Issues:

Finally, the feedback sandwich may not address underlying issues contributing to the problem. By focusing on surface-level behaviors or actions, the feedback giver may miss the root cause of the issue.

Best Practices for Using the Feedback Sandwich.

1. Structure the Feedback: When using the feedback sandwich, it's essential to structure the feedback following the positive-negative-positive sequence.

2. Choose the Right Words: Use clear, specific language that focuses on behaviors and actions rather than the person's character or personality. Avoid generalizations or sweeping statements; provide concrete examples to illustrate your points.

3. Be Authentic and Meaningful: Authenticity is vital when using the feedback sandwich. People can sense when feedback is insincere or manipulative, and it can undermine the credibility of the feedback giver.

4. Provide Follow-up and Support: Finally, it's important to provide follow-up and support when using the feedback sandwich approach. After delivering the feedback, check in with the person and ask how they are doing. Offer your support and guidance, and provide resources or training if necessary.

3.2: Assertiveness Training

Assertiveness Training and Saying No:

Many people don't like telling people they can't do something.
They may feel obligated when a colleague asks for a favor or feel pressured when someone senior needs something done.
There are even some workplaces where saying no is frowned upon, and in the police force, for example, it could be a sackable or disciplinary offense.

When 'No' Feels Impossible:

After working with people for whom saying no feels impossible [1] or just isn't allowed, we created a body of work to address it.[78]
Sometimes, it is how to say no without ever saying the word [79].
Of course, there are times when saying the n-word is a necessity.

The Consequence of Not Being Assertive:

1. You could end up staying late at the end of the day

2. You will put off your work until after you've finished everyone else's

3. You might swallow your resentment after being volunteered for something you didn't want to do

4. You may quake at the idea of having to be a bit tougher with a supplier

5. You probably avoid difficult conversations with someone you manage

Assertive or Aggressive:

So yes, aggressiveness and assertiveness may be appropriate, but there's a more excellent range of behavior choices than those two types that could be equally appropriate.

Not Nice, Not Nasty:

This leaves people with the impression that they can only do two states or behaviors: Nice or Nasty.

What can be seen with assertiveness is that it is often seen as a single form of behavior:

1. say no

2. Stand your ground

3. Be a broken record

This is quite difficult if you are genuinely unassertive or, in our jargon, simply too nice for your good.

Asserting Yourself:

The concept of asserting yourself:

1. Getting your voice heard

2. Being understood

3. Being taken into account

4. Getting your way

This needs to be broadened to include all forms of behavior. It can include:

1. Humor,

2. Submission

3. Irresponsibility

4. Manipulation

5. Playfulness

6. Aggressiveness

The critical point is that the behavior – nice, not-nice, nasty – is chosen.

We emphasize the word key because they will not be able to act until people can choose behavior free from the limiting effects of their fear of saying no and its possible consequences.

No matter how well they are taught to be assertive, they will still feel overwhelmed in difficult situations [80].

The Art of Saying No:

It is only by beginning to experience and understand how crippling these feelings can be that people can start to do anything about changing their behavior.

Therefore, when practicing 'the art of saying no,' it is wise to broaden the focus so that it isn't about becoming more assertive but changing one's behavior to fit the circumstances.

Using charm, humor, telling the truth, or even deliberate manipulation may get you what you want without attempting behavior that may go against your personality.

If you add a dash of fun or mischief, The Art of Saying No becomes a doable prospect rather than another problematic mountain to climb.

Easier Ways of Saying No:

Here are seven tips to make it easier to say 'no.'

1. Smile

If you're saying something profound, notice whether you smile or not. Smiling gives a mixed message and weakens the impact of what you're saying.

2. Stand Up

Stand up if someone comes to your desk and you want to appear more in charge. This also works when you're on the phone. Standing puts you on even eye level and creates a psychological advantage.

3. Still Your Body Language

If someone sits down and starts talking to you about what they want, avoid encouraging body language, such as nods. Keep your body language as still as possible.

4. Avoid Asking Questions

Avoid asking questions that indicate interest (such as, 'When do you need it by?' or 'Does it have to be done by this afternoon?' etc.)

5. Interrupt Them

It's all right to interrupt! Our favorite technique is to say, *'I'm sorry; I'm going to interrupt you.'* Then, use whatever tool fits the situation. If you let someone have their whole say without interrupting, they could get the impression you're interested and willing. All the while, they get no message to the contrary; they will think you're on board with their plan (to get you to do whatever...)

6. Pre-Empt Them

Saying no first. As soon as you see someone bearing down on you (and your heart sinks because you know they're going to ask for something), let them know you know: *'Hi there! I know what you want. You're going to ask me to finish the Henderson report. I wish I could help you, but I just can't.'*

7. Pre-Empt at Meetings

Meetings are a great place to get landed with work you don't want. You can see it coming. So, to avoid the inevitable pre-empt, *'I need to let everyone know right at the top that I can't fit anything else into my schedule for the next two weeks (or whatever).'* [81]

Influencing Skills:

When you make it easy for other people, they will naturally return.

By learning more effective ways of saying no, you make it more complicated for others to expect you to do what they want without considering what's going on for you. *You become more burglar-proof.*

Changing Others by Changing Yourself:

Many of us wish that the person we are in conflict with or feel intimidated by would change.

'If only' forces the other person to change how and who they are and makes them responsible for how we feel.

Using some of the tools outlined above, people can feel they are in charge of situations rather than victims of what others want.

It seems part of human nature to blame others when things go wrong or when we feel hard done by.

If you remove the 'if only' excuse, you also remove the need to blame and make the other person wrong.

What also makes it easier is that we all have to get better at 'the art of saying no'; none of us has to change our whole personalities to create a more satisfying outcome!

3.3: Role-Playing Scenarios

Although being agreeable is integral to being a team player, knowing how to say no in certain situations is also essential.

Why is it Important to Know How to Say "No Nicely"?

Following these steps can help you feel more confident and professional when you want to say "no":

1. Be Straightforward

Instead of saying *"maybe"* or *"I don't think so,"* be straightforward in your answer. Otherwise, these types of in-between answers may prompt the person to ask you the question another time.

2. Briefly Explain Yourself

It's polite to explain why you are saying "no briefly." This can help soften your answer and help the person understand why you decline. *When giving your explanation, keep it short. It's not your responsibility to give a lengthy explanation with all the details.*

3. Bring up an Alternative

If you want to be seen as a team player at work, offer an alternative when you say "no." For example, if your coworker asks for help but you're too busy, you could say, *"Sorry, no. I'm busy with my tasks right now. Please let me know if you need help by the end of the week. I can offer my help then."* This shows you want to be agreeable and helpful while respecting your boundaries.

4. Keep Your Stance

After you say "no," keep that as your final answer. By giving in and changing your answer to "yes," people may eventually get you to agree to things you don't want to do. *By staying firm on your answer, your coworkers and employer will understand they can't further persuade you.*

Here are Ten Ways to Nicely Say "No," Though There Could be Many:

Use these examples to say "no" to your employer and coworkers politely:

1."Unfortunately, I have too much to do today. I can help you another time."

2. "I'm flattered by your offer, but no thank you."

3."That sounds fun, but I have a lot going on at home."

4. "I'm not comfortable doing that task. Is there anything else I can help you with?"

5. "Now isn't a good time for me. I'll let you know if my schedule frees up."

6. " Sorry, I have already committed to something else. I hope you understand."

7. "No, I won't be able to fit that into my schedule this week."

8. "I would love to join you, but I'm feeling a little overwhelmed with work right now."

9. "I'm not taking on any other work right now. Maybe check with another department?"

10."Thank you for thinking of me, but I do not wish to accept your offer."[82]

3.4: Overcoming Cultural and Social Barriers

Teams with members from diverse races, cultures, nationalities, and religions form multicultural or cross-cultural teams. Their workplace is also multicultural, and employees can face cultural and language barriers when working in such a setting.

Cultural Barriers in the Workplace:

According to an article published by **Pennsylvania State University**, working with colleagues from distinct cultural backgrounds can help defeat cultural barriers. Here's why: you'll be able to learn about other cultures, religions, and languages. So, let's find out what cultural barriers are and how you can recognize them in the workplace.[83]

Types of Cultural Barriers in the Workplace:

Here are some of the most common types of workplace cultural barriers so you can better understand this issue.

Employees interact with each other according to their cultural standards

Work Etiquette is a term used to describe one's social behavior in the workplace. These are some habits and qualities that you can associate with work etiquette, along with examples of various cultures:

Punctuality. Getting to work or for a meeting on time varies across diverse cultures. Some cultures, like the Brits, find this quality significant and don't tolerate tardiness. On the other hand, in Brazil and Argentina, it's pretty standard to come late for a meeting, at least half an hour after the meeting starts.

Greetings. When it comes to handshakes, Singaporeans appreciate a gentle handshake that lasts around 10 seconds. In India, a handshake should be followed by greeting someone with their titles (Mr, Ms, Sir) or saying "namaste." In Brazil, they greet each other with a firm handshake or a kiss on the cheek. Apart from handshakes, in some cultures, greeting in the workplace can involve bowing—for instance, the Japanese value bowing with your back straight while your hands are at the side.

They Were Making Eye Contact. If some of your colleagues come from England, avoid making prolonged eye contact with them because you'll make them uncomfortable. At the same time, employees in South Africa tend to maintain eye contact during meetings. For them, this behavior proves that someone is focused during the meeting [1]. In addition, South Africans also nod their heads for the same reason.[84]

You are Handing out Business cards. When it comes to British culture, they usually exchange their business cards during the initial introduction. In Singapore, you must present your business card with both hands. If you find yourself at a meeting with Japanese businesspeople, remember not to throw your business cards or write on them. As for the Indian culture, it's crucial not to give or receive business cards using your left hand.

We were Making Small Talk. A casual conversation before the meeting or when it starts is quite common in India and the United Arab Emirates.

Dress Code. In India, all employees must follow a particular norm: men must wear a shirt and a tie, while women must wear sarees and salwar suits. In the United Arab Emirates, women must wear a skirt or suit below the knee. On another note, companies in Denmark usually require an informal dress code.

Work-Life Balance. In some cultures, such as Singapore, work is a priority, and employees are often expected to be responsive after work hours. At the same time, some cultures tend to maintain a better work-life balance [85]. For instance, in France, there is the Right to Disconnect Law. French employees have the right to switch off after work and are not obliged to answer any emails they get outside of working hours.

Sharing Ideas: Employees from some cultures can have difficulty sharing ideas openly.

During a loud brainstorming session in a cross-cultural team, some employees will feel uncomfortable intervening. At the same time, others will be happy to participate and share their thoughts. Now, whether you'll speak up depends on your personality, but it also depends on your cultural patterns.

For example, **Adam Goulston**, the owner of the Japanese company *Scize*, says that his team comprises Asians and Westerners. In his experience, workers find it hard to communicate during the meetings:

"I found many members of both sexes were unprepared to express themselves freely. Even if they desired to break free from the typical meetings in which the highest-ranking person does most of the talking while others listen, they were burdened by having to talk. Some even seemed humiliated by it. Perhaps it was too impulsive, or they needed more time to think or to talk with others and prepare an ideal response. The bigger the meeting, the more intense the effect."

Goulston points out that one-on-one meetings are sometimes more effective.

"In private, a shy person can feel less burdened in opening up, and a big talker can engage me in a vocal discussion."

In general, when it comes to expressing ideas and opinions, employees from individualistic cultures, like Australia or the United States, tend to share their viewpoints easily. Also, in Israel, people think that each team member is equally important and are not afraid of disagreeing with their managers.

However, workers from hierarchical cultures, such as Japan, India, and Middle Eastern countries, are accustomed to expressing their thoughts only after their senior coworkers have shared their points of view. Hierarchical standards mean a lot in Singapore, too. According to a Reddit user, only senior managers can speak at client meetings, while junior employees can only listen.

In addition, many Chinese people follow the rule of "thinking before speaking," which is why they'll have to be prepared ahead of the meeting if they're going to participate.

Personal Space: Employees perceive personal space differently across cultures. When communicating with your colleagues, you probably won't stand too close so that you won't invade their privacy. But how close is too close? Well, that depends on cultural standards.

A study [86] published in the Washington Post shows that people in Argentina and other South American countries demand less personal space than people from Asian countries. In Romania, strangers should keep their distance.

So, let's say your coworkers are from Japan and Brazil. You'll be able to stay closer to your Brazilian colleagues without making them feel uncomfortable. However, it would be best if you respected the culture of your Japanese coworkers by not standing too close to them.

Disagreement: Employees from some cultures are less likely to disagree with others.

Some cultures appreciate group harmony, so their members struggle to express their disagreements. That's because these people believe that disagreements can lead to conflicts, which disturbs group harmony. At the same time, some cultures value having a "good fight" and claim that this is a sign of trust within the culture. For instance, employees from Latin and Middle Eastern cultures usually raise their voices to reveal their arguments. However, workers from Asia and Scandinavia show their disagreement by using silence and body language. In addition, Danes are usually not afraid of disagreeing with their superiors.

Negotiation: Employees' ways of negotiating vary from culture to culture

As Erin Meyer, an author of The Culture Map, explains in the HBR article [87], *if you're negotiating with partners from other cultures, you need to be aware of particular negotiation rules.*

First of all, rules of disagreements. For instance, when someone disagrees with you in Russia, that doesn't mean that your deal is off, but *"it's an invitation to a lively discussion,"* adds Meyer. At the same time, such behavior would be a deal-breaker in Mexico. Meyer highlights that, when disagreeing, some cultures use a lot of upgraders – words like "completely" and "absolutely." This applies to Russians, French, Germans, Israelis, and Dutch. However, some cultures use downgrades "to soften the disagreement" in such situations. So, Mexicans, Thai, Japanese, Peruvians, and Ghanaians use "partially" and "a little bit."

Depending on the culture, an open disagreement can be interpreted as positive or negative. Even people from emotionally expressive cultures, like Brazil, Mexico, and Saudi Arabia, are not that keen on getting negative comments. However, for employees in Germany, Denmark, and the Netherlands, open disagreements are considered positive if expressed calmly. Look at the graph below to learn which country seems more or less emotionally expressive and ready to face confrontation.

Source:[88]

Developing trust between two negotiating parties depends on the culture, as well. Meyer says that there are two types of trust: cognitive and affective. Cognitive trust is when you rely on someone's skills, accomplishments, and reliability. Affective trust results from connecting with the other person on an emotional level. Speaking of negotiations, American culture is known for separating cognitive and affective trust. For them, mixing these two areas of trust is unprofessional. However, the Chinese are likelier to build personal connections with business partners.

Suppose you avoid asking questions requiring "yes" and "no" answers. In many cultures, like the Indonesian, it's impolite to say "no" during face-to-face conversations. Thus, they may answer affirmatively, but later, they may inform the other party of their negative response via email. At the same time, in French culture, saying "no" is acceptable when having face-to-face meetings. In their culture, this is a part of debating before the deal is closed.

They are Signing the Contract. For American culture, says Meyer, signing the contract is crucial to negotiations. Once both parties have agreed on terms, Americans seal the deal with a contract, which is a legally binding document. However, in cultures like Nigeria, offering a contract is a sign of mistrust. Nigerians rely heavily on relationships, so having a written contract isn't essential. Here's why: business people prefer flexibility in countries like Nigeria, China, and Indonesia. For them, a contract is just the beginning of a relationship. If anything changes between two business parties, their arrangements must be modified, too.

Evaluating Employees Differs Across Cultures:

Giving and receiving feedback varies from culture to culture. While individualistic cultures admire immediate feedback, even delivered in public, hierarchical cultures prefer giving and receiving feedback in a more private setting, such as a one-on-one meeting, and even in an informal environment, like outside the workplace. Also, in these cultures, praising an individual instead of an entire team can even be embarrassing for that individual. Thus, positive feedback in front of a group can decrease employee performance [89].

1. How can cultural Barriers in the Workplace be Overcome?

If you're a manager of a multicultural team, you'll need to find a way to help your employees and yourself overcome cultural barriers. Here's how you can do that.

Define what cultural behaviors are acceptable for a job and a work setting.

Not all behaviors specific to a particular culture will negatively impact your employees' performance. However, being late for work or meetings is a quality that shouldn't be tolerated, regardless of cultural background. If that's the case with your workers, be sure to let them know that, even though you respect their culture, punctuality is the company's policy.

Be Willing to Adapt:

Therefore, as their manager, be willing to get to know more about the distinct cultural standards of your employees so that you can adopt

Organize a cross-Cultural Training Program:

As Neal Goodman, a president of the consulting firm Global Dynamics Inc., points out in the article for SHRM:[90]

"We all judge everybody by our cultural lens. We have nothing else but our cultural lens. Without proper cultural training, we cannot see the situation from multiple perspectives."

Language Barriers in the Workplace:

In his famous metaphor, Claude Lévi-Strauss, the French anthropologist, connects myths and the communication process, or myths and language. For him, those involved in a communication process are like members of an orchestra. Even though each plays a different instrument, they all use the same sheet music. The result is a soothing melody.

Now, when it comes to intercultural communication (communication between diverse cultures), the musicians from the orchestra play by using not one but two musical notations (sheet music). As a result, there's an unusual melody.

To understand what each culture on your team is "playing," you must learn what language barriers exist.

What are Language Barriers?

Busineestopia defines a language barrier as *"the inability to communicate using a language."* As a result of a language barrier, people either misunderstand or misinterpret the messages.

How often do language barriers happen within companies? As stated in the research on the impact of language barriers [1] and communication style in organizational culture, 65% of companies had a problem with language barriers between companies' managers/executives and other workers. Regarding miscommunication, 67% of the respondents said that miscommunication led to inefficiency. Besides, 40% of respondents experienced complex collaboration due to miscommunication.[91]

2. Support Systems

How do You Overcome Language Barriers in the Workplace?

As a manager of a cross-cultural team, you must find a way to overcome language barriers among the employees. Here are some valuable tips.

Find an Interpreter

You should hire an interpreter to ensure mutual understanding between you and your employees from various cultures. If someone on the team speaks the language of your culturally diverse worker, be sure to use their help.

Translate all the relevant documents into your employees' native language.

Translate all crucial documents into your workers' native languages or make them bilingual to maintain a trusting relationship.

Provide Language Courses for Workers.

Let's say that your company's official language is German. Provide German language courses if you have employees from France, Slovenia, and Hungary. It will benefit them to learn particular idioms, the terminology used in the company, or some common phrases. Finally, they will feel more comfortable working in such an environment. Plus, they'll be more confident with their German language knowledge.

Use Visual Methods

If some job positions require special training and following instructions, ensure all the written material contains visual explanations, too. This is especially handy for workers from distinct cultural backgrounds, but these instructions can be helpful for all employees.

Learn the Native Language of Your Employees.
The best way to show that you appreciate your employees and their cultural diversity is by learning their native languages. As

their manager, you should learn some phrases you commonly use at work.

Wrapping Up:

Cultural and language barriers can sometimes cause misunderstandings among the employees.

However, just because you don't speak the same native language as your colleague or share the same cultural standards doesn't mean you can't bridge these barriers. Overcoming cultural differences and establishing effective communication within the team implies being willing to adapt and educating yourself through cross-cultural training and language courses.

3.5: 10 Main Takeaways

1. The Sandwich Method: This technique frames negative feedback between positive remarks, making it easier to digest and fostering a supportive environment.

2. Constructive Criticism: Balancing praise and critique encourages openness, helping individuals feel valued while receiving necessary guidance.

3. Assertiveness Training: Develop skills to confidently express your needs and boundaries without feeling guilty or pressured.

4. Understanding No: Recognize that saying no is vital for personal well-being and can prevent burnout from over-commitment.

5. Role-Playing: Practice scenarios to become more comfortable saying no in various situations, enhancing your communication skills.

6. Easier Techniques: To make the process easier, implement straightforward strategies like smiling, standing, or preemptively saying no.

7. Cultural Awareness: Understand cultural differences in communication to navigate saying no in diverse environments effectively.

8. Authenticity Matters: Be genuine in your feedback to build trust and encourage growth.

9. Follow-Up Support: After delivering feedback, check in with others to show continued support and guidance.

10. Personal Growth: Embrace the journey of learning to say no to cultivate resilience and foster healthier relationships.

Chapter 4: The Power of Boundaries

"Good fences make good neighbors."

— Robert Frost

4.1: Understanding Boundaries

1. Understanding Boundaries:

Do healthy relationships have boundaries? YES. YES. YES! All healthy relationships need boundaries. It doesn't matter if the healthy relationship is between you and your parents, children, spouse, partner, sibling, coworker, neighbor, etc. We all need boundaries to live healthy lives.

But that's much easier said than done. Far too often, we go our whole lives without establishing clear boundaries for ourselves. And it makes sense. Because if you're like me, you may believe that you need to be there and available to everyone, especially those you care about, to be seen as "good."

I was always taught that being "good" meant putting everyone else's needs before mine. I was taught that to do anything less was "selfish." And is there a dirtier word out there than "selfish?" So, when I started learning about boundaries and began to put them into place in my life, in the beginning, I felt cruel, heartless, and ashamed.

I felt like I would hyperventilate when I first tried to say, *"I understand that's what you want, but that doesn't work for me."* But that's what it takes. By the way, you will never be able to truly love yourself or prioritize your own goals if you do not set boundaries. So yes, you have to learn this skill.

There's much to be said and a lot to learn about boundaries. In this chapter, I will discuss the importance of healthy boundaries, provide examples of healthy and unhealthy boundaries, and share strategies for establishing boundaries for yourself once and for all!

What are Healthy Boundaries and Why are They Important?

Personal boundaries are guidelines, rules, or limits a person creates to identify for themselves what are reasonable, safe, and permissible ways for other people to behave around them and how they will respond when someone violates those boundaries.

Boundaries help separate us from other people. They help us craft our identity and give us space to be ourselves. Boundaries are needed to maintain your mental and emotional health, and they prevent burnout that comes from people-pleasing, being too giving, and putting everyone's needs before your own

And without clear boundaries, it's easy to forget where you end and another person begins. It's easy to forget that your decisions are your decisions, your desires are your desires, and so on.

Setting your boundaries and ensuring those around you (including your loved ones!) respect them is no small task, and it often sends people running in the other direction. So, let's discuss why they are so important.

Prevent Burnout:

When you don't have established personal boundaries (because you don't know what they are or where to start), it's easy to get burnt out saying yes to everything and everyone. Without boundaries, people and the outside world intrude. It's why houses have doors. Suddenly, your living room becomes your neighbor without a door. Without personal boundaries protecting your energy and well-being, it's easy to get sucked into feeling and believing that your energy is everyone else's energy—to be used and exploited on a whim.

Burnout is severe [92], and it cruelly affects our mental health. When burnt out, you're prone to sudden mood swings, 24/7 fatigue, exhaustion that no amount of sleep can fix, loneliness and detachment, and steady feelings of irritability, indifference, and resentment.

Being burnt out also means you're more prone to getting sick. And a stuffy nose is no cure for the grumps!

If you're a mother, I bet you've been here before. You've fed the kids, set them up in front of Paw Patrol, and now you'll step outside for five minutes. Just five minutes so you can clear your head and get back inside.

Avoid Anger and Resentment:

Eventually, burnout and stress can boil over into anger and resentment. You might lash out and find yourself not acting like your lovely, sweet self, which can easily cause guilt and shame, making you feel like a monster. This behavior can seem amplified in the eyes of your family, friends, and coworkers because they're used to you always being so lovely and saying yes to everything.

It can be shocking when you suddenly turn on them after agreeing to help them. It's like when you finally find a groove at work, but your chatty coworker knocks on your door again to tell you about their weekend, or when you're organizing a family get-together with your siblings and your sister asks you to cover the side dish she was responsible for. You find yourself thinking and then almost screaming, Leave me ALONE! Do it YOURSELF!

It's better for everyone that you prioritize your boundaries before it gets to this point. Because you don't mind helping— you love your family and friends, and making a co-worker or boss shine puts a smile on your face every time. But enough is enough! If you're running on fumes, you'll be no good to anyone [93].

Develop a Personal Identity:

Here's the truth. Without firm boundaries, you don't have any personal autonomy, which means you won't know where you start and where your family and friends begin. You're not Samantha; you're Jason's mother. You're not Brian; you're Steve's friend. You're not Lisa; you're your company's best employee.

You may be those things, but you're YOU before you are anything else.

- What do you like?
- What don't you like?
- How do you prefer people to speak to you?
- At what time of day would you prefer people to reach out to you?
- How close can people stand to you?
- What nights of the week do you prefer to go out?
- Do you prefer tea or coffee?
- Do you like to host people at your house?
- Do you like to meet up on Zoom?

These are all simple things that shape a person's personality and identity. If you don't have boundaries, you become a chameleon, changing based on whoever you're around. If you always say you don't mind, people will believe you. They'll decide what you do, what you eat, what you watch, what you read, and how often you organize the office sales contest. *Your boundaries are what make you the unique person that you are.*

It's not selfish to have boundaries, but it's selfish not to have them. If you're unwilling to care for yourself and your needs by establishing healthy boundaries, you're not helping others help you.

So come on. Say this with me:

"I am not selfish for setting boundaries."

"I am NOT selfish for setting boundaries!"

"I AM NOT SELFISH FOR SETTING BOUNDARIES!"

So, now that we know how necessary boundaries are for our health and the well-being of our friends, family, coworkers, managers, and clients, what are some healthy boundaries that we can set for ourselves?

2. What are Examples of Healthy Boundaries?

Boundaries are different than needs. It would be best to meet your needs to live a happy and fulfilling life. *Boundaries are like a line in the sand. They are declarations of the things you will not stand for.*

I have a list of boundaries that I continually add to whenever my boundaries are infringed upon. I encourage you to make a list like this, too. What essential boundaries do you want to place with the people around you? Yep—the people you love count too. The people you love are the most likely to overstep or violate your boundaries.

Here's a list of Basic Boundaries from the book ***The Verbally Abusive Relationship*** by **Patricia Evans**:

YOU MAY NOT:

1. Call me names.

2. Ridicule or belittle me in private or public.

3. Lie to me.

4. Hit me or physically hurt me in any way.

5. Be unfaithful to me.

6. Spy on me.

7. Say things purposely designed to make me doubt whether I am sane or normal.

8. Use traumas in my past to emotionally manipulate me.

9. Pressure me to cut ties with my family or friends.

10. Stonewall me—refuse to communicate.

11. Undermine me at my work or with my family or friends.

12. Attempt to turn my children against me.

13. Hurt my children in any way: physically, sexually, or mentally.

14. Be overly critical, implying I don't do anything right.

15. Force me to have sex when I don't want to.

16. Blame me for the state of your life.

17. Intimidate or threaten me.

Your list might differ, but it's an excellent place to start. What boundaries from this list resonate with you? What boundaries that are important to you are missing from this list?

Thinking about times when your boundaries were crossed is an excellent place to begin. Let's look at some signs of unhealthy boundaries.

Signs You Have Unhealthy Boundaries:

1. You don't have any time to yourself.

2. You have trouble separating your own identity from your family's.

3. You feel burnt out.

4. You lack the time and energy to pursue your dreams.

5. You say yes whenever anyone asks you to do something.

6. When you say no to anyone, you feel guilt.

7. People call you names or speak down to you, and you say nothing.

8. People in your life know how to get exactly what they want from you.

9. You think sex is your duty.

10. You feel angry or resentful when your family or someone else asks something of you.

11. You rarely set boundaries and don't know your essential boundaries.

These are unhealthy ways of living, but unfortunately, many fall into these patterns. So, how do we break free from these patterns? Let's talk about how to establish healthy boundaries in your life.

4.2: How to Establish Healthy Boundaries

You can hope that all you want is for the people around you to be respectful and have healthy boundaries, but only you can ensure you get the necessary boundaries.

Today, I will share a few essential strategies for regaining control over your life and claiming healthy boundaries with everyone, including those you love.

Identify and Prioritize Your Personal Needs

Imagine fulfilling all your needs, such as love, trust [94], safety, respect, honesty, etc. How would your life be different if you knew what and how to say it without feeling consumed by self-doubt [95]? What would it be like to feel powerful, loved, and respected all at once?

Do you know what your needs are? For some of you, the answer may come quickly. You might know immediately what your needs are. You might say, "Rhonda, I need Space, Comfort, Respect, and Support." Are those needs being met? Do the important people in your life know your needs, and do they respect them?

If unsure of your needs, consider what you need to be happy and fulfilled.

What things in life are most important to you?

What makes you want to scream or pull your hair out if you don't get it from others?

Some everyday needs include:

- Belonging,

- Respect,
- Safety,
- Acceptance,
- Friendship,
- Harmony,
- Trust,
- Commitment,
- Fairness,
- Structure,
- Joy,
- Financial Stability,
- Success,
- Community,

Once you know your most essential needs, you can start to ensure they are being met. It would be best if you did this for yourself to gain the respect and boundaries you need to live your soul's intended life.

Here's the truth. If your needs aren't being met, you are not honoring yourself and certainly not loving yourself. Here, I discuss the risk [96] of falling into anger and resentment. This WILL happen if you don't ensure your needs are met.

Repeat after me:

"My needs matter."

"My needs are important."

"My needs are just as important as anyone else's."

"I must ensure my needs are met."

It would be best if you took responsibility for meeting your own needs. If you don't, no one else will. Establishing an essential list of boundaries can help.

My Needs = Your Needs

And don't worry; this doesn't mean you won't care for others in their time of need. Taking care of my 90-year-old father-in-law recently reminded me that caring for him was tending to one of my essential needs: family. Did I give up some things to care for him for that month? Yes. And I was happy to do it because I wanted to be with him. And I was able to do that because I put boundaries in place. Boundaries kept me sane and kept my father-in-law, me, and the rest of the family on good speaking terms during a difficult time.

Establish a List of Basic Boundaries

While we might think we will remember our essential boundaries, writing them down and creating a hard list gives us something to fall back on when things get tough. When things get messy and complicated (and they always do!), you can look back on your boundaries list to ensure you aren't letting those old bad habits creep back into your life.

Your boundaries are the line in the sand that you will not allow to be crossed. What are the consequences of having your boundaries crossed? These are just as important. Depending on the boundary that's been crossed, this could mean seeing some people in your life less or cutting someone out of your life entirely. When a boss or client crosses a boundary, it could mean cutting ties with the client, looking for a new career opportunity [97], or pursuing legal action.

Rigid Boundaries: These tend to be characterized by emotional or physical distance, avoidance of intimacy, a low likelihood of asking for help, few close interpersonal relationships, protectiveness, and detachment from others.

Open Boundaries: These may include oversharing information, having trouble saying no, becoming enmeshed in other people's problems, struggling with decision-making, accepting harmful behaviors from others, and desiring to please others out of fear of rejection or abandonment.

Types of Boundaries:

Healthy boundaries can protect you from excess stress, keep your identity and values intact, reduce conflict, preserve autonomy, and maintain well-being. As you begin defining your healthy boundaries, it can be helpful to consider the different types of boundaries.

Physical Boundaries

Physical boundaries usually apply to physical space, touch, and needs. For example, you may not be comfortable shaking hands during cold and flu season. Expressing physical boundaries may sound like:

- "Hi, I prefer not to hug, but seeing you again is great."
- "Let's take a break from hiking. I need to catch my breath and have some water."

- "Welcome to my home. My room is my personal space, but if you need anything, please let me know."

Physical boundaries can be violated when you receive unwanted physical touch, your personal space is not respected, or your physical needs are denied or ignored.

Emotional Boundaries

Emotional boundaries typically concern feelings, often establishing limits on what personal information is or is not appropriate to share in various circumstances, sharing with people who respond appropriately, and limiting emotional conversations to what you can handle at that moment. Setting emotional boundaries can look like this:

- "I'm sorry to hear that happened. Thank you for sharing. I'm overwhelmed and don't think I can give this conversation my full attention. Can we return to this discussion later this week?"
- "I feel discouraged when I share my feelings and the response is accusatory. I need to share with someone who can listen without offering their opinion."

If you feel routinely drained by conversations with someone, criticized for your feelings, or asked to reveal inappropriate personal information given the context of the relationship, your emotional boundaries may have been crossed.

Sexual Boundaries

Sexual boundaries generally revolve around enthusiastic consent, respect, and understanding. They often concern how people touch, see, and treat you and what you're comfortable doing to someone else. According to Planned Parenthood, sexual boundaries may revolve around:

- Clothing: What clothes are you comfortable removing?
- Body parts: Where do you want to touch, be, see, or be seen?

Activities: What activities are you comfortable performing or participating in?

Sexual boundaries can be respected by asking for consent (which can be revoked at any time), discussing preferences, talking about sexually transmitted infection history and contraception use, and checking in frequently. Examples of setting sexual boundaries may look like this:

- "I enjoy touching over-the-clothes, but let's hold off on touching each other under our clothing. Is that something you're comfortable with?"
- "Have you had STI (Sexually Transmitted Infections) testing?"
- "I don't enjoy that, but I'd like to hear what else you might be interested in trying."

These boundaries can be violated when consent is not asked for, someone is pressured to do or see something sexual, unwanted sexual comments are made, unwanted touch occurs, or someone lies about things like contraception or sexually transmitted infections.

Intellectual Boundaries

Respecting others' opinions, thoughts, and ideas can be central to intellectual boundaries. This boundary may be crossed when someone's thoughts are dismissed or discussed in inappropriate settings. When someone crosses your intellectual boundaries, you can let them know:

- "I understand that we have different opinions, and we can discuss them later, but right now, this has become unproductive."
- "I love talking to you, but we cannot discuss politics anymore. I respect your opinions, but these conversations have become hurtful. I'd like to hear your plans for the weekend instead."
- "I cannot have another conversation about this because what you say violates my values."

Intellectual boundaries can be crossed when someone shuts down, belittles, or denies another person's thoughts or ideas.

Financial or Material Boundaries

Financial or material boundaries can establish healthy expectations for how you share money and personal possessions, who you choose to share material and financial possessions with, and how you will engage with your finances. To establish and maintain financial and material boundaries, you might say:

- "I don't lend out my car on weekdays."
- "Sure, you can borrow some clothes for the event, but I'll need them back next week."
- "I can cover your utility bills on this one occasion, but I will not give you money for vacations."

Financial boundaries can be violated when people are pressured to lend or give things or when their items are stolen or carelessly damaged.

Time Boundaries

Time can be seen as a resource, and you generally have the right to determine how to use your time. Time boundaries may reduce the risk of over-committing yourself. Consider the following examples when setting time boundaries:

- "I don't have time to talk daily on the phone, but I can set aside an hour on weekends to catch up."
- "I'd love to join you for dinner, but I can only stay for an hour."
- "I have another commitment, so I won't be able to attend the event."
- "I'd be happy to revise the project. I charge an hourly rate of ____."

When your time is violated, you may be asked to provide free professional work, spend more time with someone than you reasonably can or want to, work overtime at your job, or have little time for your needs.

Non-Negotiable Boundaries

While some boundaries may be flexible, others can be unwavering. Examples of non-negotiable boundaries may look like:

- "Having children is a priority for me. I cannot enter a long-term relationship if my partner doesn't prioritize having a family."
- "Since your dog has a history of biting, I can't let my children go over for a playdate if the dog will be indoors with them."

Non-negotiable boundaries are typically not compromised when violated and may necessitate ending relationships.

4.3: Communicating Boundaries

Boundaries are BEAUTIFUL! Learning to say no and set boundaries is a critical skill in the professional realm. It involves asserting your time, energy, and resources while maintaining positive relationships with colleagues and supervisors. Here's how you can achieve this balance.

1. Understanding the Importance of Boundaries

Boundaries are essential for maintaining a healthy work-life balance. They help prevent burnout, reduce stress, and enable you to prioritize your tasks effectively. They also establish clear expectations for your colleagues, leading to more respectful and productive interactions.

2. Self-Reflection and Prioritization

To set boundaries effectively, you need to understand your limits and priorities. Reflect on your values, goals, workload, and personal commitments. Identify what you can realistically take on without sacrificing the quality of your work or well-being.

3. Clear Communication

Clarity is critical when conveying your boundaries. Avoid ambiguous language that might be misinterpreted. Instead of open-ended statements like *"I might not have time,"* be specific: *"I cannot take on this task because it conflicts with my current priorities, which are..."*

4. Confidence in Delivery

Convey your decision with confidence. This doesn't mean being inflexible or harsh; it means having a firm yet courteous tone. Use "I" statements to express your limitations, such as *"I cannot attend the meeting at that time."*

5. Offering Alternatives When Possible

When you say no, try to provide an alternative solution. This shows that while you cannot fulfill the request, you're still supportive and willing to help find a different solution. For example, *"I can't take on this task, but I know that [Colleague] has experience in this area."*

6. Practice Makes Perfect

Saying no may be uncomfortable initially, but like any skill, it gets easier with practice. You might begin with smaller refusals and work your way up as you become more comfortable asserting your boundaries.

7. The Power of Nonverbal Communication

Nonverbal cues play a crucial role in reinforcing the message you're conveying. Maintaining appropriate eye contact and a composed posture can significantly reinforce your message when communicating your boundaries. This nonverbal reinforcement can help others take your boundaries seriously, enhancing the effectiveness of your communication.

8. Ensuring Timeliness

Communicate your boundaries as soon as possible. Delaying can lead to confusion and resentment. For example, if a deadline is unrealistic, say so at the outset, not the night before the task is due.

9. Knowing Workplace Policies

Know your workplace's policies regarding work hours, overtime, and employee rights. This information can back up your assertions when reminding others of these boundaries.

10. Building a Culture of Respect

Maintaining professionalism and respect when asserting boundaries helps foster a reciprocally respectful environment. *This means also respecting the boundaries that your colleagues set.*

11. Balancing Firmness and Flexibility

While it's essential to be firm in maintaining your boundaries, be ready to flex them when exceptional circumstances arise that genuinely warrant extra effort, as long as these exceptions don't become the rule.

12. Say No to the Request, Not the Person

Separate the refusal from your relationship with the requester. *Make it clear that it's the specific request you're saying no to, not rejecting the person or your willingness to assist with other matters.*

13. Avoid Over-Justifying

Provide a rationale, if necessary, but avoid lengthy justifications or excuses. *Over-explaining can weaken your position and invite further discussion or negotiation when inappropriate.*

14. Incorporating Technology

Use digital tools to your advantage. For instance, you can set your work chat to "Do Not Disturb" outside working hours or use auto-replies to inform colleagues when unavailable.

15. Preparing for Pushback

Be prepared for some resistance, especially if you're beginning to assert your boundaries more than you have in the past. *Stand your ground respectfully and reiterate your position if needed.*

16. Modelling Behaviour

Lead by example. *When you respect your boundaries, you signal to others that they should do the same. This can* cultivate a work environment where everyone's time and contributions are valued.

17. Identifying Chronic Boundary Crossers

Watch for individuals who consistently ignore or test your boundaries, and prepare specific strategies for addressing these situations. This may include having more in-depth conversations about respect and expectations.

18. Consulting with Leadership

If necessary, discuss your boundaries with your supervisor or human resources. They can provide support and guidance on how to enforce your boundaries within the framework of company policy.

19. Self-Care as a Priority

Prioritize self-care and mental health. When you're well-rested and mentally refreshed, you're more likely to be productive and able to maintain professional relationships effectively.

20. Continuous Evaluation

Regularly review your boundaries to ensure they are still appropriate and effective. As your role evolves, so too may your limitations and needs.

4.4: Overcoming Boundary Violations

What are Some Warning Signs that Your Boundaries are Being Crossed?

Sometimes, we're unsure if our boundaries are ignored or violated, especially if we like or respect the other person. We may feel something is wrong, but we can't say what is bothering us.

These examples of boundary-crossing behaviors may help you put a name to what behaviors might be concerning to you:

- Not listening to you when you say "No",
- Controlling who you are friends with or getting upset when you spend time with people they don't like,
- Wanting or demanding access to your phone or your social media accounts,
- Asking you to do something that goes against your morals, values, or beliefs,
- Making you feel guilty for not fulfilling their needs,
- Expecting you to go everywhere they go, even if you don't want to,
- Telling other people personal things you have shared with them,
- Lying to you,
- Stealing from you,
- Taking advantage of you, such as always having you pay for meals,
- Telling you what to wear or getting upset when you wear something they don't like,

- Touching your body without permission - this includes when you are sleeping if you are intoxicated, or unable to give consent in any other way.

Boundaries are your limits about what you feel okay with physically and emotionally. You might hear people refer to boundaries as your "personal bubble" or the "wall" you keep between you and things that make you feel unsafe. Only YOU can decide where and when someone has crossed your boundaries.

Every person is different in where their boundaries lay, and one person may feel that something or someone crossed their boundaries while another person may not feel the same. For example, one person's boundary may be that they are not okay with hugs from other people, but they feel comfortable with a handshake or a fist bump.[98]

How to Deal with Repeat Boundary Violations?

One of the biggest challenges people face when setting boundaries [99] is dealing with repeat boundary violations.

No matter how hard you try or how skilled you are at setting boundaries, you may encounter some people who repeatedly violate your boundaries.

You can't make people respect your boundaries.

Unfortunately, manipulative, selfish, and low-self-esteem people tend to violate personal boundaries repeatedly.

So, what can you do? How can you cope with chronic boundary violators? There isn't a one-size-fits-all answer. Let's begin by considering some variables to help you discern the right approach for your situation.

Things to consider when dealing with repeat boundary violations

Who is violating your boundaries, and how much power do they have?

The relationship's nature, power differential, and closeness make a difference. Your response to your mother will differ from your response to your boss, which will differ from your response to your neighbor.

Is the Boundary Violator Willing to Change?

Is s/he willing to work with you to improve the relationship? Is s/he willing to go to counseling? Is s/he sensitive to your needs or feelings?

How Long Has This Been Going On?

More extended behavior patterns are more complex to change (but undoubtedly possible when someone is motivated).

Has the Boundary Violator been Physically Aggressive?

Safety is paramount. You must proceed cautiously if the person violating your boundaries has been violent or threatened. I highly recommend getting help from supportive people, professionals, and law enforcement.

Are you a Minor?

If you're a child, you must ask an adult for help. Reach out to an adult at school or church, a friend's parent, or a hotline. You do not need to figure this out alone!

Are you Genuinely Setting Clear, Consistent Boundaries?

Generally, people tend to overestimate the strength of their boundaries. Understandably, sometimes you back down, feel tired, overwhelmed, or scared, and don't follow your boundaries. Just like setting rules with children, boundaries don't work when they are only enforced sometimes. Boundaries must be evident and consistent when dealing with someone who doesn't respect you. Such a person is looking for holes in your boundaries and using them against you. So, assertively tell them this behavior is not OK and follow through with consequences.

Now, let's move on to the original question of what to do when someone continues to violate your boundaries.

How do we Deal with Repeat Boundary Violations?

1. Continue to set solid and consistent boundaries. I know this seems obvious and redundant. However, this is the part of setting boundaries that you control. You don't control how people respond and can't force people to respect your boundaries.

2. Write it Down.
Record the boundary violations and your responses. This will help you check for weak spots in your boundaries. If you notice that you aren't consistently setting healthy boundaries, make

adjustments. And if you are being very consistent, writing it down will help you decide if you can accept these violations.

3. Be Clear about what treatment you'll accept and what you won't.

People also tend to set a boundary in their minds and then allow it to be pushed back. For example, I knew a woman who, years prior, had told herself that she wouldn't tolerate her husband coming home drunk and cursing at her anymore. By the time I met her, her husband was coming home drunk several times per week, regularly cursing at her in front of their children, and he'd slapped her once. This is far beyond what she thought she'd put up with. It helps to write down your boundaries and say them out loud to a supportive person who will help you stay true to them.

4. Accept that Some People Will Not Respect your boundaries no matter what you do.

This is a brutal truth to accept because we'd like to be able to force people to respect our boundaries. I know it isn't enjoyable to realize that you may have to decide whether you want to continue to have a relationship with someone who doesn't respect your boundaries. But you can't change someone else's behavior. You can choose to accept it, or you can choose to disengage.

5. Detach from the Outcome.

It's tough to do. One way to detach from someone who repeatedly violates boundaries is to stop responding in the same old ways. Some people intentionally violate boundaries to hurt you, get a reaction out of you, and exert control. Don't engage in the same old arguments with these people. You can ignore or laugh off their comments and not show them it hurts you. This shifts the power. (This doesn't apply to someone physically harming you.)

6. Decide to Limit or cut off all Contact.

Suppose Great Uncle Johnny makes you feel uncomfortable by standing too close and making sexually charged comments. In that case, you can decide not to attend family gatherings at his house, attend but not be alone with him, or avoid seeing him again. You have choices.

Particular challenges when dealing with repeat boundary violators.

You Live with the Boundary Violator.

Let's imagine that you're living with Great Uncle Johnny while you go to school in San Francisco, and there's no way that you can afford to move out. You might identify these choices: Quit school and move back home. Stay out of the house as much as possible (study at the library and coffee shop, come home late, and leave early). Ask your friends if you can spend the weekends with them. Get a second job and save money so you can move out. None of these choices seem ideal, so you must trust your instincts and do your best.

The Boundary Violator Holds a Position of Authority.

This is perhaps the most complex situation of all. It can be scary and dangerous when a parent, teacher, boss, law enforcement officer, or anyone in authority violates your boundaries. Please consider whether it would help to get someone else involved (perhaps this person's superior). I realize that life is complicated, and sometimes, doing so can worsen things, particularly in the short term. Again, it would be best to make some difficult decisions about whether you can stay away from this person, limit contact, or avoid being alone with them.

Others pressure you to stay or minimize your feelings or the harm you've experienced.

When you decide that you need to make changes to a relationship due to boundary violations, not everyone will be supportive. This is not the time to be a people-pleaser. It's unhealthy to stay in contact with someone who causes you harm to make someone else happy. Don't continue living at Great Uncle Johnny's because your dad says you're overreacting and "that's just how Johnny is." Maybe your dad has a perfectly respectful and pleasant relationship with Uncle Johnny. Or maybe he's oblivious to how Uncle Johnny treats you. There are infinite reasons for your dad to say this. The point is, it doesn't matter. You are uncomfortable, and you need to honor that.

You Love and Care About the Boundary Violator.

The boundary violator is often a parent, spouse, or someone you care about. It's much easier to detach or walk away from someone you don't love deeply. However, you can't abandon yourself and let your love for another lead you to accept disrespect and mistreatment.

But setting boundaries is a form of self-love and self-respect. If you don't love and respect yourself, others won't either.

You can ask your loved one to engage in a process of change with you, such as family counseling, going to a support group, or reading a book about boundaries. They tell you they don't intend to change if they refuse or don't follow through. And you are once again faced with needing to decide if it's healthy to continue the relationship as is or with modifications.

Suppose you are the one who loved his aging mother, but she was verbally abusive and intrusive with her questions. She criticized everything her son did to help her. He couldn't bear to cut her out of his life, but he was miserable before, during, and after each visit. His way of dealing was to hire someone to help with her day-to-day care and limit his visits to once a week. Whenever his mother began criticizing him, he told her she was being critical and hurtful and cut the visit short. This was the best solution he could come up with.

People will keep asking, demanding, and taking from you until you learn when and how to say no.

All too often, our "yes" comes from a place of fear [1]. We are scared of what will happen if we say no. We're afraid people won't see us as kind and selfless. We're afraid of the response we'll receive back. We're afraid our self-esteem will diminish if we aren't able to give everything to our loved ones. We're afraid our family won't love us as much if we say no. [100]

We want to Say Yes Because We Want to be the Hero.

We want to be the favorite sister who dropped everything to help with a move or the favorite employee who always goes the extra mile for their client and never turns down extra work from their boss.

For Your Health and Well-being, you must be able to say no, even (especially!) to those you love. Saying yes all the time leads to fatigue, stress, irritability, and burnout. And in the end, what you were trying to avoid will happen. You will become unpleasant, unhappy, and unhealthy, alienating and pushing away the people you care about most. This is why it's so important to learn to say no.

Try this. Next time you are asked to do something, stop and think about it first. Say you will get back to that person tomorrow. Yes. Tomorrow... Don't give up your time that easily by answering "yes" immediately. Consult your calendar first. Can you realistically fit something else into your calendar? Next, take a deeper look at your own goals. Will their ask infringe on your own needs, goals, or health?

How Do You Respect Healthy Boundaries for Other People?

Good work! If you're still here, you're sticking right with me. Boundaries are so important, which is why this is a long read. But there's one more thing I want to cover: other people's boundaries.

Why is it important to respect the personal boundaries of others? Other people need their boundaries respected just as much as you do. Now that you have a better understanding of just how important they are, you can get better at honoring the boundaries of those around you.

How Can You Do This?

Here are a few pointers to follow:

- Actively listen to others. Please pay close attention to the words they choose and pay even closer attention to their body language. Even if they say yes to something, their body language may indicate that they mean no.
- If you ask someone if they can help you with something, give them the space to say no.
- If you invite someone to an event, give them time to think about it before demanding an answer.
- Ask people if they need more space.
- When sharing your needs and boundaries, ask the people you care for about theirs, too.
- Don't insert yourself (without being asked) into problems that don't involve you.
- Stop trying to control everyone around you. They need to be able to make their own decisions.
- Watch for signs of burnout in the people you care about.

Healthy people respect boundaries, and they ensure their boundaries are enforced. I encourage you to pay close attention to your boundaries. Set essential boundaries and adhere to them—by the way, boundaries can only be if there are consequences when your essential boundaries are crossed. It's in your best interest and those around you if you are given the time and space to craft your identity, manage your health, and practice self-care.

You Don't Need to Go It, Alon

Setting healthy boundaries and sticking to them is tough, especially when it's been so long since you had any. Many of us have never had healthy boundaries, as we were never taught them. It's time for that to change [101

4.5: 10 Main Takeaways

1. Importance of Boundaries: Healthy relationships require boundaries, which are essential for maintaining emotional and mental well-being.

2. Avoiding Burnout: Establishing boundaries prevents burnout by protecting your energy and helping you manage personal demands.

3. Preventing Anger and Resentment: Clear boundaries can reduce the anger and resentment arising from overcommitting and neglecting one's needs.

4. Personal Identity: Boundaries help you maintain your individuality, allowing you to express preferences and needs without losing yourself in relationships.

5. Understanding Healthy vs. Unhealthy Boundaries: Recognizing differences is crucial; healthy boundaries enhance relationships, while unhealthy ones can lead to stress and conflict.

6. Strategies for Establishing Boundaries: Identify your needs, list essential boundaries, and communicate them effectively to those around you.

7. Empowerment: Setting boundaries is not selfish; it is a necessary act of self-care that empowers you to lead a fulfilling life.

8. Identifying Boundary Violations: Recognizing warning signs—like someone ignoring your "no" or demanding personal access—is vital for maintaining emotional safety.

9. Coping with Repeat Violations: Consistent boundary-setting is critical. Document violations and responses to identify weaknesses in your boundaries.

10. Choosing Healthy Relationships: Sometimes, you must decide whether to limit or cut contact with those who disrespect your boundaries, prioritizing your well-being over others' expectations.

Chapter 5: The Art of Assertiveness

"The most common way people give up their power is by thinking they don't have any."

— Alice Walker

5.1: Defining Assertiveness

Do you often feel you fail to get your opinions heard, or do people readily dismiss or undermine your views? Maybe you have a habit of handling situations aggressively or lack the confidence to speak up.

You might have felt unable to do anything about it then, but by learning to be more assertive, you can stand up for yourself and become a strong and confident communicator.

In this chapter, we'll look at why assertiveness is necessary and explore some strategies that you can use to become more assertive to further both your confidence and influencing skills.

What Is Assertiveness?

Assertiveness is a critical skill that can help you better manage yourself, people, and situations. It can also help you influence others to gain acceptance, agreement, or behavior change.

It is the ability to express one's opinions positively and confidently. Assertive people are in control of themselves and are honest with themselves and others.

Assertiveness vs. Aggression

It's not always easy to identify assertive behavior. There's a fine line between assertiveness and aggression; people often confuse the two. For this reason, it's helpful to define the two behaviors to separate them.

Assertiveness is based on balance. It requires being forthright about your wants and needs while still considering the rights, needs, and wants of others. When assertive, you are self-assured and draw power from this to express your point firmly, somewhat, and empathetically.

Aggressive behavior is based on winning. You do what is in your best interest without regard for other people's rights, needs, feelings, or desires. When you're aggressive, the power you use is selfish. You may come across as pushy or even bullying. You take what you want, often without asking.

So, a boss who dumps a pile of work on your desk the afternoon before you go on vacation and demands that it be done straight away is being aggressive. The work needs to be done, but by dumping it on you at an inappropriate time, they disregard your needs and feelings.

When you, on the other hand, inform your boss that the work will be done but only after you return from vacation, you hit the sweet spot between passivity (not being assertive enough) and aggression [102] (being hostile, angry, or rude). You assert your rights while recognizing your boss's need to get the job done.

The Benefits of Being Assertive

Being assertive lets you communicate your wants and needs more authoritatively while remaining fair and empathetic. It can also help you become more self-confident and improve your mental health. [103]

Assertiveness provides several other benefits that can help you in your workplace and other areas of your life. In general, assertive people:

Make Great Managers. They get things done by treating people fairly and respectfully and are treated by others similarly. This means they are often well-liked and seen as leaders with whom people want to work. [104]

Negotiate Successful "Win-Win" Solutions. They recognize the value of their opponent's position and can quickly find common ground with them.

Are Better Doers and Problem Solvers. They feel empowered to do whatever it takes to find the best solution to their problems.

Are Less Anxious and Stressed. They are self-assured and don't feel threatened or victimized when things don't go as planned or expected. [105]

They have greater job satisfaction. They feel confident saying "yes" to the person and "no" to the task and maintaining boundaries.

The Risks of Being Assertive

Some organizational and national cultures prefer people to be passive and may view assertive behavior as rude or offensive. *Research has also suggested that gender can affect how assertive behavior is perceived, with men more likely to be rewarded for being assertive than women.* [106]

However, this doesn't mean you should succumb to the status quo! Instead, be bold while avoiding naivety.

There is also a risk that you could go too far. If you become too assertive, you may stop listening to others despite their excellent ideas. This will only act to alienate your colleagues and damage relationships. *Avoid this by experimenting with small steps at first until you find what works for you in your workplace. A little assertion at the right time can be a highly effective way of developing your profile and self-esteem.*

5.2: Developing Assertiveness Skills

Becoming more assertive is not always easy, but it is possible. So, if your disposition or workplace tends to be more passive or aggressive than assertive, then it's a good idea to work on the following areas to help you get the balance right:

1. Value Yourself and Your Rights

To be more assertive, you must gain a good understanding of yourself [107] and a strong belief in your inherent value and value [108] to your organization and team.

Self-belief is the basis of self-confidence [109] and assertive behavior. It will help you recognize that you deserve to be treated with dignity and respect, give you the confidence to stick up for your rights, protect your boundaries [110], and remain true to yourself, your wants, and your needs.

Tip:

While self-confidence is essential to assertiveness, you must ensure it doesn't develop into a sense of self-importance. Your rights, thoughts, feelings, needs, and desires are just as necessary as everyone else's but not more important than anyone else's.

2. Voice Your Needs and Wants Confidently

If you're going to perform to your full potential, you need to ensure that your priorities—your needs and wants—are met.

Don't wait for someone else to recognize your need—you might wait forever! Take the initiative and start identifying the things that you want now. Then, set goals so that you can achieve them.

Once you've done this, you can tell your boss or colleague precisely what you need from them to help you achieve these goals clearly and confidently. And don't forget to stick to your guns. Even if what you want isn't possible right now, ask (politely) whether you can revisit your request in six months.

Find ways to make requests that avoid sacrificing others' needs. *Remember, you want people to help you, and asking for things in an overly aggressive or pushy way is likely to put them off doing this and may even damage your relationship.*

3. Acknowledge That You Can't Control Other People's Behavior

Don't assume responsibility for how people react to your assertiveness. If they, for example, act angry or resentful toward you, try to avoid reacting to them similarly.

Remember that you can only control yourself and your behavior, so do your best to stay calm and measured if things get tense. *You can say or do what you want if you respect and do not violate someone else's needs.*

Tip:

The LADDER mnemonic is an effective way of assertively resolving problems.

4. Express Yourself in a Positive Way

It's important to say what's on your mind, even when you have a complicated or harmful issue. But it would be best if you did it constructively and sensitively.

Don't be afraid to stand up for yourself and to confront people who challenge you and your rights. You can even allow yourself to be angry! But remember to control your emotions and to stay respectful at all times.

5. Be Open to Criticism and Compliments

Accept positive and negative feedback graciously, humbly [111], and positively.

If you disagree with the criticism you receive, you need to be prepared to say so without getting defensive or angry. The Feedback Matrix [112] is a great tool that can help you see past your emotional reactions to feedback and instead use it to achieve significant, positive change.

6. Learn to Say "No"

Saying "no" can be difficult, especially when you're not used to it, but it's vital to becoming more assertive.

Knowing your limits [113] and how much work you can take on will help you manage your tasks more effectively and pinpoint any areas of your job that make you feel like you're being taken advantage of.

Remember that you can't possibly do everything or please everyone, so you must protect your time and your workload by saying "no" when necessary. When you have to say "no," try to find a win-win solution [114] that works for everyone.

7. Review Your Progress

Whenever you try assertiveness, ask yourself, "*How did I handle that?*" "*What did I do well?*" "*What might I do differently next time?*" This will keep you on track and help you identify development areas.

If you experience a setback, don't let it deter you. Instead, try to learn from it. It is essential to recognize your successes and keep your failures in perspective.

5.3: Assertive Communication Techniques in Different Directions

In addition to the above strategies, there are several simple but effective communication techniques that you can use to become more assertive. These are:

"I" Statements

Use "I want," "I need," or "I feel" to convey bare assertions and get your point across firmly. For example, *"I feel strongly that we need to bring in a third party to mediate this disagreement."*

Empathy

Always try to recognize and understand [115] how the other person views the situation. Then, after considering their point of view, express what you need from them.

Say "No" Firmly and Calmly.

Saying "no" and then waffling about your preferences or your capacity suggests that your "no" can be massaged into a "yes." Being respectfully yet assertively definitive when you decline the request is the first step toward maintaining your boundaries.

Use the Word "No" as the First Word of Your Response.

"I don't think I can get to it" can easily be perceived as "maybe I can get to it"—the exact scenario you're trying to avoid. An unemotional "no" at the beginning of your answer shows resolve and respectful, firm assertiveness.

Give a Brief, Apparent Reason for the Refusal.

"I have an urgent deadline that cannot be rescheduled" is not easy to argue against. Make your reason for saying "no" reasonable yet unbreakable, and keep it brief enough to suggest you get going now. This conversation won't be long.

Avoid Long Excuses or Justifications.

"I have all these meetings, and I need a little time between them, and I have a lunch appointment, and then I have to make a phone call." It sounds busy, but it also suggests you know how to open windows in your busy schedule to accommodate unscheduled requests. Stay calm and on point. Emotion, either from the perspective of pain or anger, undercuts your logical argument for declining the request. "I'm only one person!" can easily lead to an apology and "yes" after an extended emotional conversation. *Take a breath, stay composed, and be concise and definite.*

Suggest an Alternative for Satisfying the Request.

If there's a reasonable alternate solution to the request that you can propose, do so. It will assuage any guilt you may feel; hopefully, the person who made the request will appreciate it. It can also decrease the likelihood that declining the request will return later to haunt you.

Boycott the Words "I'm Sorry."

Most of us naturally apologize when declining a request or demand, but in doing so, we set a trap for ourselves and signal a weakness to the person making the request. You can say "no" and still be a nice person. Stay strong!

Be Consistent in Words, Voice, and Body Language.

Inconsistency also conveys weakness and indecisiveness. This opens the territory to a counter-argument in the other person's favor, meaning you've allowed them to take one more step toward breaking through the boundary you've set.

Reinforce the "No" Message Through Eye Contact.

Few visual cues are more effective at letting someone know you mean what you say than direct, uninterrupted eye contact. Go ahead—you can do it!

Escalation

If your first attempts at asserting yourself have been unsuccessful, you may need to escalate the matter further. This means becoming firmer (though still polite and respectful) with the person you request help from. It may also involve *telling them what you will do next if you aren't satisfied, such as starting the disciplinary process.*

However, remember that you may still not get what you want regardless of the consequences you communicate to the person in question. If this is the case, you may need to take further action by setting up a formal meeting [116] to discuss the problem or escalating your concerns to Human Resources or your boss.

Ask for More Time

Sometimes, it's best not to say anything straight away. You might be too emotional or not know what you want yet. *If this is the case, be honest and tell the person you need a few minutes to compose your thoughts.*

Change Your Verbs

Try using more definite and emphatic verbs when communicating. This will help you send a clear message and avoid "*sugar-coating*" your message so much that people are left confused by *what you want from them.*

To do this, use verbs like *"will"* instead of *"could"* or "*should,"* "*want*" instead of "*need,"* or "*choose to*" instead of "*have to."*

For Example:

"I will be going on vacation next week, so I will need someone to cover my workload."

"I want to attend this training course because it will help me progress in my role and career."

"I choose this option because I think it will be more successful than the other options."

Be a Broken Record

Prepare the message that you want to convey ahead of time. If, for instance, you can't take on any more work, be direct and say, "*I cannot take on any more projects right now.*" If people still don't get the message, keep restating your message using the same language and don't relent. Eventually, they will realize that you mean what you're saying.

Tip:

Be careful with the broken record technique. Please use it to protect yourself from exploitation. But it can be manipulative and dishonest if you use it to bully someone into taking action that's against their interests.

Scripting

It can often be hard to express your feelings clearly and confidently to someone when you need to assert yourself. The scripting technique can help here. *It allows you to prepare what you want to say in advance, using a four-pronged approach that describes:*

1. The Event. Tell the other person exactly how you see the situation or problem. *"Janine, the monthly production costs are 23 percent higher than average. You didn't indicate this, meaning I was completely surprised by the news."*

2. Your Feelings. Describe how you feel about the situation and express your emotions clearly. *"This frustrates me and makes me feel like you don't understand or appreciate how important financial controls are in the company."*

3. Your Needs. Tell the other person precisely what you need from them so they don't have to guess. *"I need you to be honest and let me know when we start going significantly over budget on anything."*

4. The Consequences. Describe the positive impact that your request will have on the other person or the company if your needs are met successfully. *"If you do this, we will be in a good position to hit our targets and may get a better end-of-year bonus."*

Key Points

Being assertive means finding the right balance between passivity (not assertive enough) and aggression (angry or hostile behavior). It means having a solid sense of yourself and your value and acknowledging that you deserve to get what you want. *And it means standing up for yourself even in the most challenging situations.*

Assertiveness doesn't mean dominating or dismissing others to get what you want. *Acting in your interest without considering other people's rights, feelings, desires, or needs is aggression.*

You can learn to be more assertive over time by identifying your needs and wants, positively expressing them, and saying "no" when needed. *You can also use assertive communication techniques to help you communicate your thoughts and feelings firmly and directly.*

It likely won't happen overnight, but practicing these techniques regularly will slowly build the confidence and self-belief you need to become assertive. You'll also likely become more productive, efficient, and respected.[117]

5.4: Overcoming Barriers to Assertiveness

Assertiveness isn't just a skill but the foundation of excellent communication and leadership. However, many hesitate to speak up confidently, fearing being perceived as difficult or rude. This concern often holds us back from asserting ourselves effectively. Similarly, we also want to ensure that our attempts to be assertive don't inadvertently cross the line, maintaining respect and understanding.

Understanding Your Barriers

To effectively overcome barriers to assertiveness, it is crucial to identify and understand the unique psychological, social, and cultural factors contributing to these obstacles. *Assertiveness is often misconstrued as aggression, yet it is fundamentally about respectfully and clearly expressing one's thoughts, needs, and boundaries.*

Psychological barriers can stem from a lack of self-esteem or deep-seated beliefs formed during childhood that one's needs are less important than those of others. Social factors, such as gender norms and societal expectations, further complicate the ability to assert oneself, with individuals often facing criticism or backlash when defying traditional roles. *Culturally, the value placed on harmony and collectivism over individual expression in some societies can deter assertive behavior.*

Understanding these barriers requires a multifaceted approach that acknowledges the complexity of human behavior. It involves acknowledging the legitimacy of one's feelings and rights while also considering the impact of external influences. This analytical and empathetic approach paves the way for tailored strategies that address specific barriers, empowering individuals to navigate through and ultimately overcome them, fostering a sense of control and self-assurance.

Strategy One: Self-Reflection

The first strategy for overcoming barriers to assertiveness involves engaging in self-reflection. This process allows individuals to critically examine their thoughts, emotions, and behaviors to understand the root causes of their passivity. This reflective approach is not just about identifying weaknesses; it's a constructive method to uncover personal strengths and areas for growth, facilitating a path toward assertive communication [118].

Self-reflection can be Structured into Four Key Areas:

1. **Identifying Emotional Triggers**: Recognize situations or interactions that evoke discomfort or fear, leading to passive behavior. Understanding these triggers is the first step in managing responses more assertively.

2. **Assessing Beliefs and Values**: Evaluate the beliefs and values that underpin reactions to these triggers. Some may find that a deep-seated belief in avoiding conflict at all costs inhibits assertive behavior.

3. **Reflecting on Past Interactions**: Analyze past instances where passivity prevailed over assertiveness. What were the consequences? This retrospective view can highlight the cost of non-assertiveness and motivate change.

4. **Acknowledging Strengths:** It's crucial to recognize existing assertive qualities and successes. This boosts self-esteem and serves as a foundation to build more assertive behaviors.

Through this analytical and empathetic approach, individuals gain a deeper understanding of their assertiveness barriers, equipping them with the insight necessary to initiate meaningful change.

Strategy Two: Skill Building

Building upon the foundation of self-reflection, skill building emerges as a critical next step in enhancing one's assertiveness. This process focuses on practical techniques and exercises to develop this crucial competency. *The journey toward assertiveness is not purely introspective; it requires the deliberate cultivation of specific skills that empower individuals to communicate their needs, boundaries, and opinions effectively and respectfully.* This process involves learning to express oneself clearly and confidently without resorting to aggression or passivity.

Evidence-based approaches suggest that structured training programs that include components like active listening, the use of 'I' statements to express feelings and needs without placing blame, and techniques for maintaining composure under pressure can significantly benefit assertiveness skill building [119]. *These skills are not innate but acquired through practice and dedication, highlighting the importance of a systematic approach to skill development* [120].

Moreover, empathetic communication is a crucial aspect of assertiveness. Understanding others' perspectives and responding with empathy does not diminish one's assertiveness; rather, it enhances the effectiveness of assertive communication [121] by fostering mutual respect and understanding. Through dedicated skill building, individuals can transform their approach to interactions, leading to more positive outcomes in both personal and professional contexts.

Strategy Three: Practice

Having developed a foundation in assertiveness skills, individuals must practice consistently to refine and integrate these abilities into their daily interactions. This crucial stage demands dedication and a structured approach to ensure the newly acquired skills are theoretically understood and become a natural part of one's communication repertoire. Practice bridges knowledge and application, and its importance cannot be overstated.

To Effectively Incorporate Assertiveness Practice into Daily Life, Consider the Following Steps:

1. Set Realistic Goals: Start with small, manageable situations where you can apply assertiveness. Incremental progress builds confidence [122] and competence.

2. Seek Feedback: Engage trusted peers or mentors who can provide constructive feedback [123] on your assertiveness techniques. This outside perspective is invaluable for growth.

3. Role-Play Scenarios: Simulate challenging interactions with a friend or coach. This safe environment allows for experimentation and adjustment of your approach.

4. Reflect on Experiences: After assertive encounters, analyze what worked and what could be improved. Reflection solidifies learning and fosters adaptability.

These structured steps facilitate a gradual yet impactful integration of assertiveness into one's behavior, empowering individuals to navigate their social and professional environments with greater confidence and control.

Overcoming Setbacks

Despite the structured approach to assertiveness practice, individuals may encounter setbacks that challenge their progress and require strategies for effective resolution. Overcoming these setbacks is crucial for sustaining the journey toward assertiveness. *Research suggests that setbacks often arise from internal barriers, such as fear of conflict or rejection, and external factors, like unsupportive environments. Recognizing these as part of the learning process is the first step toward managing them.*

Empirical evidence underscores the importance of reflection in overcoming setbacks. This involves identifying the specific nature of the setback, understanding its impact, and strategizing on how to address it. *For instance, if fear of conflict is a recurrent barrier, cognitive-behavioral techniques can be employed to reframe negative thought patterns associated with assertiveness.*

Moreover, seeking feedback from trusted peers or mentors can provide valuable perspectives and encourage resilience. Studies in organizational behavior highlight that constructive feedback [124] fosters adaptability and growth, essential components in mastering assertiveness.

Lastly, setting small, achievable goals post-setback can rebuild confidence and momentum. This incremental approach ensures steady progress while minimizing the likelihood of future setbacks. Through these targeted strategies, individuals can navigate and overcome setbacks, reinforcing their path toward assertiveness with resilience and determination.

Frequently Asked Questions

1. **How Does Cultural Background Influence One's Ability to Be Assertive, and What Specific Approaches Can Address This?**

Cultural background significantly influences an individual's assertiveness, shaping communication styles and self-expression norms. It is paramount to recognize and respect these cultural nuances.

Tailored approaches, such as culturally sensitive assertiveness training and inclusive dialogue practices, can effectively bridge these gaps.

2. **Can Assertiveness Be Misunderstood as Aggression, and How Can One Ensure Their Assertiveness Is Perceived Correctly?**

Assertiveness may indeed be misconstrued as aggression, potentially leading to misunderstandings in communication. To ensure assertiveness is perceived accurately, clear, direct language combined with an open, non-confrontational tone is essential. *Active listening and empathy towards others' viewpoints also play a crucial role.*

Employing these strategies can help clarify intentions and foster a respectful dialogue, ultimately enhancing the effectiveness of assertive communication [125] in achieving desired outcomes.

3. Are There Any Physiological Techniques, Such as Breathing Exercises, That Can Support Assertiveness in High-Pressure Situations?

Yes, physiological techniques can significantly bolster assertiveness in high-pressure situations.

For instance, deep breathing exercises help manage physiological responses to stress, enabling a calmer and more composed demeanor. This can facilitate more transparent communication and assertive behavior.

Additionally, practicing mindfulness can improve emotional regulation, allowing individuals to respond rather than react impulsively.

Such techniques, grounded in evidence-based research, offer practical tools for enhancing assertiveness while maintaining control and professionalism.

4. How Does One Maintain Assertiveness in Virtual Communication Settings, Such as Emails or Video Conferences, Where Body Language Cues Are Limited?

Maintaining assertiveness in virtual communication settings demands a nuanced approach. *One should leverage clear, concise language and assertive tone to navigate the absence of physical cues and ensure messages are unambiguous.*

Utilizing structured formats and emphasizing key points can enhance clarity. Additionally, actively seeking feedback and engaging in follow-up communications can bridge the gap left by reduced non-verbal interactions.

This strategy fosters an environment of assertiveness, even in the virtual realm, empowering individuals to communicate effectively [126] and confidently.

5. What Role Does Mental Health Play in Developing Assertiveness, and Are There Any Particular Mental Health Challenges That Make It More Difficult?

Mental health significantly influences one's capacity for assertiveness, both as a facilitator and a barrier. Conditions such as anxiety and depression can severely impede an individual's ability to assert themselves due to increased fear of confrontation or diminished self-worth.

Conversely, positive mental health can enhance self-confidence and communication skills [127], crucial for assertive behavior. Addressing these mental health challenges is vital for developing and maintaining assertiveness.

Final Thoughts

In conclusion, surmounting the barriers to assertiveness requires a multifaceted approach that encompasses understanding personal obstacles, self-reflection, honing necessary skills, and consistent practice.

Overcoming setbacks along this journey necessitates resilience and a commitment to personal growth [128].

As an allegory, one might consider the process akin to navigating a labyrinth, with each turn representing a challenge overcome and every dead end a lesson learned. This ultimately guides one towards the coveted center: assertive communication.

This endeavor, though arduous, is instrumental in fostering self-confidence and enhancing interpersonal relationships.[129]

5.5: 10 Main Takeaways

1. **Understanding Assertiveness**: Assertiveness involves expressing your opinions positively and confidently, balancing your needs with others.

2. **Assertiveness vs. Aggression**: Distinguish between assertive behavior, which respects others, and aggressive behavior, which prioritizes self-interest.

3. **Self-Value**: Recognizing your worth is essential for assertiveness. Understand that you deserve respect and should assert your rights.

4. **Confident Communication**: Voice your needs and goals to others without waiting for recognition.

5. Control Your Reactions: You can only control your behavior, not others. Stay calm and respectful, regardless of their responses.

6. Positive Expression: Constructively confront issues, express feelings, and maintain respect while being assertive.

7. Acceptance of Feedback: Embrace criticism and compliments positively to foster personal growth.

8. Saying "No": Master "no" to protect your time and workload while seeking win-win solutions.

9. Consistent Communication: Use consistent words, tone, and body language to reinforce assertiveness.

10. Continuous Improvement: Regularly review your assertiveness progress to identify successes and areas for growth.

Chapter 6: Embracing Self-Care

*"To keep the body in good health is a duty...
otherwise we shall not be able to keep our
mind strong and clear."*

— **Buddha**

6.1: The Importance of Self-Care

"In the hustle of the day,
Amid the tasks that come your way,
Find a moment, still and clear,
To hold yourself a little near.
Begin the morn with gentle grace,
A quiet time, a slower pace.
Breathe in deep, let worries cease,
In the morning light, find your peace.
Set aside a space and time,
A sacred spot, your sublime.
In busy hours, take a break,
For your health, for your own sake.
Embrace the stillness, meditate,
In calm and quiet, reinstate.
A balance sought, a mind at ease,
In mindful moments, tensions freeze.

Nourish yourself with food that's pure,
With water clear and rest assured.
Exercise, let your body move,
In every step, your spirit grooves.
Create a ritual, soft and kind,
A bedtime tale to soothe the mind.
In restful sleep, renew, restore,
Wake each day to love some more.
Boundaries set, learn to say no,
In self-respect, let limits show.
In saying no, you claim your right,
To self-care moments, day and night.
Indulge in hobbies, passions true,
In creativity, renew.
Read a book or paint, or play,
In joy and laughter, find your way.
Surround yourself with love and care,
In strong friendships, your burdens are shared.
For in the weave of life's grand art,
Self-care begins within your heart.
So, every day, in every part,
Prioritize your own dear heart.
In care and calm, in love's embrace,
You'll find your peace, your sacred space."

This is a poem written by **Prachyyyy**
Masters in Computer Applications @ MIT WPU, Pune
[130]

This is a poetic expression about what self-care is.

Ask yourself:

- When the chips are down who do you want to be with?
- How do you want to be remembered when you're gone?
- How do you want to make a difference in the world?
- Is the pursuit of material wealth worth the strained relationships that are left on the path?

Adulthood is overrated. A great many people utter this statement out of frustration, and it's not surprising. Being an adult sometimes comes with overwhelming responsibilities. There are targets to meet at work and a lot of work to do at home. When you factor in social activities and other engagements, you will relish the opportunity to trade places with that baby with nothing to worry about. But we all know that's next to impossible. *The only way to be at peace with yourself is by embracing the numerous responsibilities and focusing on what is essential. This includes self-care.*[131]

Be enough for yourself first; the rest of the world can wait! This statement is sufficient to state that self-care or self-love is essential to life. If your compassion doesn't include you, what purpose can it *serve?*

Self-care is essential for everyone. Everyone should learn to take care of themselves and love themselves. Some may call it selfish. There is no harm in being selfish, but be selfish for your body, skin, mind, and soul. Materialistic deeds won't take you anywhere, but self-care will *definitely*.

Scientists and researchers have even proven that no one can live a happy and healthy life without self-care or self-love. Self-love might seem hard to achieve, but it's not unachievable. There are many ways to practice self-care.

So, let's learn more about it. We will be discussing:

What is Self-Care or Self-Love?

Self-care or self-love is about nurturing or honoring yourself in the best possible ways. Self-love isn't just about saying that you love yourself. It's more than that. It's about understanding your worth, body, mind, and *soul*.

It's all about you, but it means taking control of your life and doing what's best for your mind, body, and happiness. This can include physical activities such as running, bicycling, yoga, exercise, dance, and so on, or relaxing activities such as reading, eating your favorite food, *or taking a warm bath.*

Self-care is about caring for physical and mental health and putting yourself first. It's a doorway to a good, healthy life. It makes your body healthy. *When your body and mind feel healthy, you start shining in your daily activities.*

For instance, you will find many people around who are super confident while dressing up or super energetic while giving presentations in the office. What makes them so happy about themselves? It's all self-care and self-acceptance. *For them, self-care is the mantra of living a happy life. They feel motivated, confident, happy, and assertive all the time.*

That's obvious. When you love and care for yourself, goodness, luck, and happiness find their way toward you. You attract them; you manifest them. *Some people even say that doing self-care is like manifesting happiness. Once you become happy and self-aware, you become successful.* It teaches you to live life fully and handle and overcome failures with a smile. You feel liberated!

Why is Self-Care Important? What are the Benefits of Self-Care?

Self-care is the way to look after yourself. When you believe in self-care and practice it, you produce positive feelings that boost motivation, confidence, and self-esteem. Self-care gives you energy and creates an aura around you that helps you support yourself and others.

It's even clinically proven that practicing self-care eliminates depression, stress, and anxiety, improves concentration and confidence, and increases happiness, energy, and more.

We live in a society where we must prove ourselves daily by working long hours, caring for everyone around us, doing daily chores, and more. *While working out these, we forget to look into the mirror and ask ourselves, when was the last time we had pampered ourselves?*

There is nothing wrong with taking some time out for yourself and engaging in some self-care practices. It helps to relieve daily life pressure, reset your mood, and get back to the healthy point where you can feel pampered and energized. You don't need anyone else to do it for you. You only have to do it yourself. After all, it's all about you!

The concept of self-care became more prominent during the pandemic. People were stuck in their homes, looking for ways to stay calm and happy. *The single foremost reason that people don't participate in self-care practices is time.*

And, during the pandemic, everyone had plenty of time. At that time, people understood the importance of self-care and the benefits they could have with it. Now, somehow, it has become the trend. *We won't mind making it a trend until it's helping everyone.* So, let's know more about why self-care is important:

Importance and Benefits of Doing Self-Care: Helps You to Perform at Your Best

Technically, self-care is meant to create balance in your life. It's a way to address all the concerns hampering your mind, body, and soul. It's all about addressing the issues that affect your body and mind and taking the time to work them out and nourish them. People who practice self-care tend to be stress-free and live a higher quality of life. It helps you *perform at your best.*

Boosts Self-Confidence and Self-Esteem

Self-care is essential for building inner strength. It encourages the way you think about your mind and body - your worth. Once you channel it, you become more confident and build self-respect. In our busy lives, we compromise our mental health and wellness, which leads to life's inevitable curveballs. *Following self-care can give you the strength to fight against inevitable circumstances by bringing out your best.*

Opens Your Mind and makes you aware of Your Personal Needs

Self-care is all about becoming aware of what your body and mind desire. Once you start following self-care practices, you become aware of your needs and look for the best ways to support them. In short, it's a kind of awareness program revolving around your body's needs, mental peace, *and spirituality.*

It makes you feel Energized.

Practicing self-care reduces stress and increases mental clarity. It has endless benefits, such as increased energy, better communication with confidence, better sleep, a sense of purpose, and more.

Makes You Resilient

Self-care practices help you to honor yourself mentally and take you to a better place to confront any challenge and stress with a smile. It builds resilience. *If you keep on stressing and carrying the stress on your body, it can manifest hypertension or muscle tension, making it challenging for your body and mind. Following self-care helps to outlet the stress and make a way for your wellness.*[132]

The Benefits of Self-Care Include:

Healthier Relationships: Taking care of yourself first is an important, though overlooked, aspect of being able to take care of others. You may be surprised how energy invested in yourself can produce more incredible energy to invest in the people around you and healthier relationships overall.

Improved Physical Health: Self-care practices pack a punch against heart disease, stroke, and cancer, with researchers finding reduced rates of these disorders in those who regularly practice it.

Higher Self-Esteem: It makes sense that if we invest time and resources into things that increase our self-esteem and make us feel more relaxed, capable, and organized as human beings, we'll feel better about ourselves.

Improved Discipline: Not only do we reap the direct benefits of our self-care methods, but we also gain vital mental fortitude from witnessing ourselves doing things that are good for us that we might not always want to do at the moment.

Here Are Some Tips for Self-Care to Improve Your Well-Being:

1. Pay Attention to Your physical health

Physical health is a core part of self-care. The body and the mind have a unique connection, and it isn't easy to be in high spirits when you are not feeling good about your body. *Research has shown that regular exercise increases the level of serotonin in our body, significantly improving mood and energy. When exercising for self-care, you should choose an activity you love. It could be a regular run, brisk walking, swimming, or anything else that makes you feel alive. You derive extra fulfillment from doing what you love, and it is the love that encourages persistence even when it seems you do not have time for it.*

2. Get Enough Sleep

Too many people are sleep-deprived, and it takes a toll on their physical and mental health. We seem to have taken the maxim 'hard work pays' too seriously. We now spend so much time working and very little time sleeping. Sleep scientists recommend that adults need at least 6-8 hours of sleep every night. Your body needs time to rest and renew. Daytime naps are also excellent for refreshing our bodies *and improving concentration levels.*

3. Be a Healthy Eater

Your diet is a significant part of self-care, an aspect you should be wary about. *When you ask people about foods that make them feel good, you get answers like a juicy steak, mounds of lasagna, or incredibly delicious cupcakes. However, consistently indulging in these delicacies is NOT self-care. Healthy, nutritious foods are one of nature's best gifts to us. Make a habit of consuming good foods that build your body.*

4. Identify the Things that Matter to You

This may seem easy, but it can be challenging to practice. To identify the things that matter most, ask yourself the tough questions.

5. Change Your Mindset / Gratitude

Too often, we focus on the negatives while showing little appreciation for the beauty around us. It's what happens when you have a bad breakup; all you can remember is how badly the person hurt you. We tend to forget all the fantastic things that the relationship brought us. Cherish the good memories and hold them dear, even if the unpleasant ones attempt to consume you. Show gratitude and appreciation for the little gifts in life. Take time to be still and meditate more. If you can adopt a gratitude mindset, you are on your way to achieving the highest level of self-care.

6. Incorporating Self-Care into Daily Life

Making self-care a priority requires conscious effort and intention. Here are some practical tips for incorporating self-care into your daily routine:

- **Start with Small Steps**: Identify activities that bring you joy and relaxation and allocate time for them regularly.
- **Create a Self-Care Routine**: Develop a schedule that includes self-care activities and treat them as non-negotiable appointments with yourself.
- **Practice Mindfulness**: Be present in the moment and engage fully in your chosen self-care activities.

- **Set Boundaries**: Learn to say no to activities or commitments that overwhelm you and prioritize your well-being.
- **Seek Support**: Contact trusted friends, family, or professionals for assistance or guidance. [133]

Live Your Best Life

Self-care is personal, and no general principle will always work. What motivates you and inspires you is different than the person next door. Look for the things that make you feel alive. Make dates with yourself, and when you commit to working out or doing something for yourself, keep the commitment you make to yourself. We don't back out on our friends; we don't back out on ourselves. By being healthy about self-care, you will feel better equipped to help others. Go live your best life.[134]

6.2: Types of Self-care

Nathan Brandon, Psy.D., a licensed clinical psychologist based in San Francisco, defines self-care as actively protecting and promoting physical, mental, and emotional health.

A recent review in the International Journal of Nursing Sciences describes it as "the ability to care for oneself through awareness, self-control, and self-reliance to achieve, maintain or promote optimal health and well-being" and points out three common attributes:

Self-awareness is essential for the person to attend to their needs.

Self-control, or the ability to regulate and process emotions.

Self-reliance denotes confidence in the capacity to take on external challenges.

Dr. Brandon says self-care is essential because it helps us stay healthy and balanced in many areas. *"It allows us to manage stress, prevent burnout, and maintain our overall well-being."*

He adds that self-care can be done with or without the support of a healthcare professional. While it "doesn't replace professional help, it does provide additional options."

How Can You Practice Self-Care Without Therapy?

Self-care is often an integral and encouraged part of regular therapy sessions, says Dr. Brandon. *"Therapists can teach coping skills that can be used for self-care,"* he says. *"For example, mindfulness and relaxation practices are often taught to people with anxiety to give them tools to manage their symptoms outside of therapy."*

It can also be helpful and can be learned without professional guidance. *"[Self-care] can provide support and help prevent or manage mental health difficulties,"* he says.

"For example, self-care practices such as exercise, relaxation, and mindfulness can help reduce stress levels."

Self-care [135] is paramount for everyone, whether they're in therapy or not, adds **Sam Zand**, ***D.O., a clinical psychiatrist and chief medical officer in Las Vegas and co-founder of the mental health platform Better U***. "Self-care can be just as helpful as therapy, if not more because we practice it daily and we're focusing on our present and building a better future," he says.

Practical Types of Self-Care

Self-care can look different from person to person, and no quintessential playbook applies to everyone. What makes you feel good and best supports your overall mental, physical, and emotional health can change depending on many factors, including your needs and the challenges you face at any given time.

Dr. Zand says practicing self-love is the foundation of any successful self-care practice. Once we feel at peace with ourselves, we can improve our relationship habits, set reminders to be present to our loved ones, *and build boundaries and standards for our interactions."*

9 Types of Self-Care & How to Practice

We wear many hats in our daily lives. We clock in for work, sweat it out at the gym, corral clutter at home, wrangle the bills, catch up on the news, and even snag a late-night

Netflix episode. These different tasks can deplete us, but they have just as much potential to revitalize us if we infuse them with self-care.

Here are nine different types of self-care:

1. Emotional Self-Care

Emotional self-care [136] gives your inner emotions room to breathe and voice themselves. Have you ever found yourself repressing what you feel in everyday life? Or wearing a mask in social situations? Or maybe even denying the emotion that you're experiencing? Yep, we've all been there. And bottling up your feelings or repressing anger [137] usually doesn't end well.

What should you do instead? *Allow yourself moments to tune in to how you feel.* For example, if you are feeling stressed about an upcoming project, don't run away from this feeling. Have an honest internal dialogue with yourself instead, and allow yourself to express the feeling however you need to. Admit the emotions that are present and calmly accept their existence.

Below are Examples of Emotional Self-Care:

- Journaling [138]
- Practicing positive daily affirmations [139]
- Using a gratitude app [140]
- Enjoying laughs with friends
- Talking through your emotions with a therapist

2. Financial Self-Care

If you want to get technical, money is the substance that takes care of your basic needs. But it understandably causes a lot of stress for some of us! *Financial management as a form of self-care might seem a new idea at first, but after reflecting on how much anxiety money issues can cause, it can make a lot of sense.*

Setting aside time to map where your money is going, reflecting on your spending priorities, and determining what needs to be done to reach your financial goals are all ways of taking care of yourself. *Many people find these tasks queasy to contemplate but feel relieved after completing them. In addition, feeling more secure and knowledgeable about money can help prevent sticky situations such as financial abuse* [141].

Below are examples of financial self-care:

- Setting aside money for investments each month,
- Using an app to help track your finances,
- Utilizing a financial professional when you need guidance,
- Setting financial goals for yourself (monthly, yearly, and so forth),
- Cutting out unnecessary expenses.

3. Spiritual Self-Care

For many, spirituality and religion are essential avenues for mental restoration and continuity. *Spiritual self-care habits can give individuals a crucial sense of structure and meaning, providing a space to let go of anxieties and fears. While religiosity is one avenue of spirituality, it is hardly the only one.*

For some, spirituality can be as simple as communing with nature or practicing meditation [142]. Whatever form it takes for us, it holds both grounding [143] and healing potential in the rush of our busy lives.

Below are Examples of Spiritual Self-Care:

- Meditation,
- Listening to religious music,
- Daily devotional/religious reading,
- Joining a religious community,
- Participating in an outdoor yoga class.

4. Professional & Academic Self-Care

It's common for our jobs or educational careers to sap up most of our energy during the workday, leading to either work or college burnout. *We're inundated by new tasks, the pressure to perform, and the various financial entanglements of these duties. In the ambitious, career-centered land of America, it can be challenging to set boundaries and carve out pockets of self-care around these obligations.*

Choosing a satisfactory work-life balance takes careful effort, but the benefits are worth it. More energy, less stress, and greater confidence to handle new demands will likely come our way. And guess what? When this happens, we have more attention to give to the other domains of our lives (and they're equally important)!

Below are examples of professional self-care:

- Setting specific office hours,
- Making a realistic, manageable daily agenda,
- Saying 'no' to extra projects you don't have time for
- Recognizing and celebrating your small accomplishments
- Trying the Pomodoro time-management technique

5. Mental Self-Care

Once we leave the cozy confines of our educational institutions, it can become quite easy to neglect "staying sharp." Many low-grade digital diversions compete for our attention spans at every moment. However, we also know that mental self-care, such as spending time learning something new or stretching our brains in new ways, can nurture our intellectual curiosities and, in turn, enrich our lives.

Below are examples of mental self-care:

- Listening to a podcast,
- Doing a crossword puzzle,
- Reading a thought-provoking book,
- Engaging others in conversation about topics you would love to learn more about,
- Visiting museums and historical sites.

6. Physical Self-Care

We're well-acquainted with the importance of self-care when our bodies become physically sick. We pay extra attention to getting adequate sleep, staying hydrated, and feeding ourselves nourishing foods. What if we extended that sense of physical self-care and attention to the rest of our lives? For some of us, exercise is vital to our daily routine.

Regular exercise has a host of psychological benefits besides keeping us limber. Endorphins rush, anyone? Even if hitting the gym isn't your thing, a relaxing evening walk may be. Physical self-care isn't limited to exercise, either. Something as simple as prioritizing a skincare routine also fits into this realm. Whatever helps maintain or rejuvenate our bodily mechanics can be considered valuable physical self-care.

Below are examples of physical self-care:

- Joining a workout class,
- Taking a daily walk with your significant other, kids, or dog,
- Staying up-to-date on regular doctor, dentist, and optometrist appointments,
- Scheduling an occasional spa day,
- Setting a healthy sleep schedule.

7. Environmental Self-Care

Self-care indeed entails gaining some mastery over our bodies and minds. What we often forget, however, is the extent to which we can master our environments as well! The cool thing is that when we focus on environmental self-care, we care for the things around us, and in turn, *we inadvertently care for ourselves.*

Environmental self-care can be a powerful self-soothing tool. It's also a helpful starting point when focusing on ourselves feels too daunting. It can take the form of practical, straightforward steps that benefit those around us, too.

Below are examples of environmental self-care:

- Doing a quick house tidying-up before going to bed,
- Assigning regular monthly or quarterly organizational tasks (cleaning out closets, junk drawers, paper stacks, and so forth),
- Organizing digital files, emails, and notes regularly,
- Making dinnertime a priority, tuning out distractions, clearing the table, lighting a candle, and so forth,
- Making the bed every morning.

8. Recreational Self-Care

Stepping away from our many roles and responsibilities throughout the day and making time for recreational self-care, such as our hobbies and pastimes, is vital to nurturing our inner lives. *Many fall prey to assuming that we don't "deserve" such avenues and can push our recreations into the future, believing them to be indulgent "extras."*

Your recreation choices may vary, but never be afraid to prioritize them. Your creativity can affect mental health; you may desperately need this outlet! *Some may gain considerable psychological fulfillment from their professional work lives, while others may need to turn to their recreational pursuits to achieve the same satisfaction.*

Below are examples of recreational self-care:

- Watching a favorite movie,
- Painting, drawing, or sculpting,
- Playing a team sport,
- Gardening,
- Baking a fun treat.

9. Social Self-Care

Relationships with other humans have been part of life since our very beginnings. We all need social self-care and time with other humans, but we all differ in the amount and type of social interaction we desire. *Introverts may prefer more alone time, and their self-care may look like saying 'no' to one social invite too many and spending the evening alone to avoid introvert burnout.*

On the other hand, extroverts may require some weekend socializing as a vital means of relaxation and recharging for the week ahead. Social self-care can entail building meaningful relationships, mending strained relationships, and ending potentially damaging ones.

Below are examples of recreational self-care:

- Joining local MeetUp groups,
- Planning a fun weekend with friends,
- Setting healthy boundaries in relationships,
- Ending toxic relationships,
- Setting phone reminders to avoid forgetting to check in with friends [144]

6.3: Creating A Self-Care Plan

A self-care [145] plan is a personalized, intentional approach to managing your well-being and a commitment to treating yourself with kindness and compassion. It can be flexible and evolve with your needs. It involves identifying what you need to thrive physically, mentally, emotionally, and spiritually and outlining actions or routines that help you meet those needs.

Recognizing your unique stressors and joys can help you craft self-care strategies that work for your wellness. By recognizing that your well-being [146]is essential in taking care of yourself, you'll be better equipped to face life's challenges and support those around you.

The Benefits of a Self-Care Plan & Why You Should Create a Self-Care Routine

Self-care [147] strategies aren't all about indulgence. They can build resilience, happiness, and overall health. Having a self-care plan can help with the following:

- Enhancing physical health,
- Reducing stress and anxiety,
- Improving mental health,
- Boosting self-esteem and self-compassion,
- Encouraging a healthier work-life balance,
- Promoting emotional resilience,
  We are strengthening relationships.

How to Make Your Self-Care Plan a Habit You'll Stick to?

Turning a new self-care routine into a lasting personal wellness habit can be challenging, but with the right approach, it's entirely achievable.

Start Small

The key to forming new habits is to start small [148] and gradually increase the complexity or duration of your self-care activities. If you want to exercise more, begin with short, 10-minute walks and slowly build up to longer sessions. *This approach makes the task more manageable, increasing your likelihood of sticking with it.*

Include Activities You Enjoy

Choose self-care activities that bring you joy [149] and relaxation. If you enjoy nature, consider adding a weekly hike to your plan. If you love reading, dedicate time to unwind with a book each evening. *When self-care feels like a treat rather than a chore, you're more likely to maintain the habit.*

Set Reminders

Set reminders on your phone or write them in your planner in the early stages. These prompts can help keep you accountable [150] and ensure you don't forget your self-care activities amidst a busy schedule.

Be Flexible

Some days will be busier than others, and unexpected obligations may arise. If you miss a self-care activity, don't be too hard on yourself, but look for ways to adapt your plan.

Build Slowly Over Time

Consider adding more once you successfully incorporate one or two self-care activities into your routine. Building self-care strategies slowly can prevent overwhelm [151] and make your routine more sustainable.

Keep it Fun

Experiment with different activities to keep your routine fresh and exciting. The more you look forward to your self-care time, the more likely you prioritize it.

Reflect on Your Progress

Take time to reflect on how your self-care routine is impacting your life. Notice any improvements in your mood [152], stress levels, or overall well-being to motivate you to continue.

Seek Support

Share your self-care goals with friends or family for additional motivation and accountability. You might even find a self-care buddy to share activities and celebrate achievements, making the process more enjoyable and supportive.

How to Create Your Own Self-Care Plan in 7 Steps

To create a personalized self-care plan, reflect on your current lifestyle, identify your needs, and address those needs through deliberate actions. A self-care plan can include many activities and practices, from simple daily habits like staying hydrated and getting sufficient sleep to personalized strategies such as setting boundaries, engaging in hobbies, or practicing mindfulness [153] and meditation [154]. Include activities that refresh and rejuvenate you physically, mentally, and emotionally.

Most importantly, a self-care plan is designed to evolve as your life changes, allowing you to adapt to new challenges and priorities to support your overall well-being.

1. Assess Your Current Situation

Evaluate your daily routines [155], work-life balance, physical activity, diet, social interactions, and stressors to understand which aspects of your life need the most attention.

2. Identify Your Needs

Pinpoint your specific needs [156]. Where do you need more support or improvement? Is your physical health lacking exercise or a good diet? Are you emotionally drained and needing stress management strategies? Be specific about what you need to feel balanced and fulfilled.

3. Brainstorm Activities to Meet Your Needs

List activities that can help you achieve your goals. Only include activities you enjoy or find meaningful, as this will make incorporating them into your routine more manageable. For physical health, activities might include walking, yoga [157], or joining a dance class. Consider journaling, therapy sessions, or creative outlets like painting for emotional well-being.

4. Set Clear, Achievable Goals

Considering your current lifestyle and commitments, ensure your goals [158] are specific, measurable, and realistic. *If you focus on improving your physical health, a goal might be to exercise for 30 minutes thrice a week. You might aim to practice 10 minutes of mindfulness meditation daily for emotional well-being.*

5. Schedule Your Self-Care Activities

Add your chosen activities to your daily or weekly schedule. Be intentional about carving out time for self-care, just as you would for any other necessary appointment. *Consistency is vital, but flexibility is also essential. Life can be unpredictable, so be prepared to adjust your plan as needed.*

6. Monitor Your Progress and Adjust as Necessary

Regularly reflect on your self-care journey. What's working well? What challenges are you facing? Are there activities you don't enjoy as much as you thought you would? Make changes to your plan so it works for you.

7. Seek Support When Needed

Share your self-care goals with friends or family members who can offer support, encouragement, and accountability. *If you're struggling to meet your goals, consider seeking help from professionals, such as therapists and other healthcare professionals, for tailored guidance.*

6 Key Pillars of a Self-Care Plan

Focusing on different areas of your life can help you create a balanced approach to self-care. Not every pillar will require the same attention, so tune into your current needs and adjust your focus to support your wellness. However, you're feeling.

1. Physical Care

Looking after your body might include exercising regularly to boost your mood and overall health, eating [159] well to fuel your body and mind, getting adequate rest and sleep [160] for recovery and well-being, and seeing your doctor regularly to address or prevent health issues.

Physical care can directly impact your energy levels, mood, and ability to engage in other self-care strategies.

The Daily Move [161] from Mel Mah is a great way to incorporate mindful movement into your practice.

2. Emotional Care

Practices that help you understand, express, and manage your emotions can include journaling to process feelings, seeking therapy or counseling for more resounding emotional support, practicing self-compassion [162] and kindness, or developing coping strategies for stress [163] and anxiety [164]. You can enhance your resilience, mental health, and relationships by prioritizing emotional care.

The Calming Anxiety [165] breathing meditation can help you cope with big feelings.

3. Social Care

Nurturing relationships is essential for our mental and emotional health. To cultivate a sense of belonging, support, and connection, consider spending quality time with friends and family, building and maintaining supportive relationships, engaging in community activities or groups that align with your interests, and setting healthy boundaries [166] to protect your well-being.

4. Spiritual Care

Spiritual care is your connection to something greater than yourself, whether through religion, spirituality, or personal beliefs about purpose and existence. Spiritual care can include meditation [167], prayer, time in nature [168], or pursuing activities that provide purpose, calm, and fulfillment.

5. Intellectual Care

Keeping your mind engaged and stimulated can involve reading, learning new skills, following creative pursuits, or doing any activity that challenges you and sparks curiosity. Intellectual care can contribute to cognitive health [169], personal growth, and accomplishment.

6. Professional Care

For many, professional fulfillment [170] can be a significant part of overall well-being. A meaningful, satisfying career, seeking balance in work demands, and setting goals for professional development can help support your emotional and mental health.

Self-Care Plan FAQs

Can Self-Care Plans Change Over Time?

Self-care plans are intended to evolve as you do. As your circumstances change, so will your self-care needs. Regularly reassessing your plan allows you to adapt to life's transitions and ensure your self-care practices remain relevant and supportive to meet your needs and promote your well-being [171].

How Often Should I Engage in Self-Care Activities?

Ideally, self-care should be a daily practice, but the frequency and type of activities can vary depending on your personal needs, schedule, and the specific goals of your self-care plan. Some practices, like mindfulness or gratitude journaling, can be done daily to help improve your mental health. Others, such as physical exercise or social events, might be scheduled weekly. The key is making self-care a regular part of your routine.[172]

Is it Okay to Include Activities Like Hobbies in My Self-Care Plan?

Hobbies and activities you enjoy are excellent elements of a self-care plan. *Hobbies can provide a sense of joy, relaxation, and fulfillment essential for positive mental health and overall well-being.* Whether painting, gardening, or playing a musical instrument, any hobby that brings you happiness [173] can be valuable for stress relief and mental wellness.

What Should I do if I Struggle to Stick to my Self-Care Plan?

Struggling to stick to your self-care plan is common, especially when life gets busy or stressful. If you find yourself facing this challenge, consider simplifying your plan.

Focus on one or two manageable activities that you find most beneficial and enjoyable. Reflect on any barriers preventing you from prioritizing self-care and explore ways to overcome them. It's okay to adjust your plan to make it work for you. Seek support from friends, family, or professionals for encouragement and accountability with your wellness.

Can Self-Care Plans Help with Mental Health Issues?

Self-care plans can play a significant role in managing mental health issues by providing strategies to cope with stress, anxiety, and depression. Activities focused on relaxation, stress management [174], and emotional well-being can offer significant relief and support. However, while self-care is essential for mental health maintenance, seek professional treatment if you have a severe mental health condition.

Calm your Mind. Change Your Life.

Mental health is complex, but getting support doesn't have to be. The Calm app puts the tools to feel better in your back pocket, with personalized content to manage stress and anxiety, get better sleep, and feel more present.

6.4: Overcoming Obstacles to Self-Care

Google searches for "Self-Care" have quadrupled in the last five years. But what exactly is self-care? Why is society in desperate need of it? And what prevents us from taking care of ourselves?

While there are many definitions of self-care, the concept is simple: take part in an activity that nourishes your mental, emotional, or physical well-being. It can be difficult, however, to actively incorporate this practice into our routines when the days are short, and our "to-do" lists are long.

Exploring How Gender, Class, Race & Religion Can Create Barriers to Self-Care

According to the ***UK's Mental Health Foundation, Black, Asian, and Minority Ethnic communities (BAME)*** "understand and talk about mental health in different ways." In some cases, "mental health problems are rarely spoken about and can be seen in a negative light," which ultimately discourages people from seeking help.

There is work to be done to destigmatize self-care within different cultures, both within and outside of these communities. Internally, the challenge is not to convince "believers" that self-care is essential; it's about proving to "non-believers" that their mental health and well-being are worth discussing, prioritizing, and caring for. Externally, we need to work on amplifying the importance of managing your mental health and well-being for people of color.

Patrick Watt, *Commercial Director of BUPA (The British United Provident Association Limited) Global*, highlighted that for many people, the imagery and role models used in marketing self-care reinforce the misperception that it is only relevant to certain socio-economic classes or those already interested in meditation and mindfulness. *We need more diverse voices in the wellness community, from practicing psychologists to campaign spokespeople, who bring credibility, expertise, and shared experiences to the table.*

Focusing on the 'Self' Often Creates Feelings of Shame

When you deconstruct the phrase "self-care," the first word has a somewhat negative connotation in this context, while the latter is undoubtedly positive. Research supports that selfishness differs from self-care, so distinguishing those two things is essential. *Remember that putting your oxygen mask on before helping others is valuable.*

Expanding the Meaning of Self-Care & Mindful Activities

One of the biggest challenges of integrating self-care practices is choosing an activity that doesn't feel forced or cliched. Broadening the definition of self-care frees us to choose habits and hobbies that we can easily incorporate into our lives.

Finding the balance between committing to something and not adding another stressful task to our "To Do" lists is essential. What matters is awareness of how a particular act of self-care makes you feel and whether it results in positive emotions and outcomes. Having an activity you can mindfully embrace reduces the reluctance to prioritize and perform it.

Focusing on the Long Term & Forgetting Immediate Gratification

One major deterrent to self-care is that we often seek assistance during a crisis. Self-care must be a consistent, incremental, and cumulative effort to yield the best results— the vitamin versus the paracetamol. If we only take care of ourselves in the middle of a storm, we deprive ourselves of the ability to approach challenges with a clearer mind. We can also rush into solutions that may only have a temporary impact. We must be "patient and gentle with ourselves" during times of great anxiety and take a moment to think about what we truly need. When we're in a rush, we make fewer desirable decisions... undermining the power of self-care and deterring us from seeing its true potential.

Improving Workplace Culture & Shifting Societal Standards

We can't discuss self-care without examining the impact of the workplace on our mental health. Over the past 30 years, advancements in technology have created round-the-clock expectations to be on. We are inundated with emails, calls, meetings, messages, and deadlines from increasing numbers of platforms. *As a society, we have adapted to information overload but also suffered the consequences. The focus must be on the interplay between workplace culture and broader societal norms and how these entities shape our commitment.*[175]

The Human Journey

While we tend to think of medical professionals as healthcare providers, most of all, care is provided by people for themselves and their families. Increasing our competence and confidence in self-care may be the most essential function of any healthcare system.

The Hidden Health Care System

When the healthcare system is described, patients are often viewed primarily as passive healthcare consumers and health professionals as active providers of services to improve health. *The usual image of the healthcare system is a pyramid with specialists (e.g., surgeons, oncologists, radiologists, etc.) at the top and primary care (e.g., family practice, internal medicine, pediatrics, etc.) at the bottom. This incomplete image of the healthcare system is, in reality, only the segment for professional care. Professional care is just the tip of the iceberg, with the much larger system of lay health care or self-care submerged beneath the surface and hidden from view.*

Consider that 75% of the general population experiences some physical discomfort or symptom in any month. Between 70% and 90% of these symptoms are self-diagnosed and self-managed without the help of health professionals. If only 10% of these individuals were to forgo self-care and seek professional care, the demand for costly medical care would increase by nearly 50%, immediately swamping the healthcare system.

At the same time, it is estimated that at least 25% of physician office visits are for problems that patients could treat themselves. If self-care increased by even a tiny percentage of this amount, such as 5%, the demand for expensive professional services could be reduced by nearly 25%. This suggests that it may be possible to improve health while reducing healthcare costs simply by helping patients to care for themselves, i.e., knowing when to seek professional advice and when and how to use self-care.

The Bottom Line: *Primary healthcare providers are not doctors or nurses. Instead, they provide health care for themselves and their families.*

Once consumers are viewed as providers of care, practical and safe self-care methods could be developed and disseminated. A vital function of the healthcare system then becomes increasing self-care competence and empowering patients to become active partners in healthcare.

Many developing and developed countries are harnessing the power of lay people as providers of care, such as "Anganbari" in India. People are being trained to be health workers and health coaches to assist others in the communities with self-care, healthy lifestyle changes, and how to effectively access professional medical and social services when needed and appropriate. Increasingly, lay people informally and formally provide health care with good health and economic results.

Where There Is No Doctor

Millions worldwide lack access to quality professional medical care due to geographic, economic, and cultural barriers. Village health workers equipped with carefully selected and curated health information can often help these people make better self-care decisions.

One group providing such resources is the Hesperian Foundation, a nonprofit organization offering over 20 health guides spanning women's health, children, disabilities, dentistry, health education, HIV, and environmental health. Available in more than 85 languages with scores of clear illustrations, these materials are used in 221 countries and territories, from Afghanistan to Zimbabwe. Hesperian health guides are used by community health workers, Peace Corps volunteers, missionaries, teachers, health educators, and community organizers to improve health worldwide. Hundreds of government agencies and nonprofit organizations rely on these guides to provide practical and comprehensive information that moves communities to take action on various health issues – from disability rights to women's health, from protecting local ecosystems to training the next generation of health workers.[176]

Self-Care Credo

- Health care is not only everyone's right but everyone's responsibility.
- Informed self-care should be the primary goal of any health program or activity.
- Ordinary people with explicit, straightforward information can prevent and treat most common health problems in their homes—earlier, cheaper, and often better than doctors.
- Medical knowledge should not be the guarded secret of a select few but should be freely shared by everyone.
- People with little formal education can be trusted as much as those with a lot. And they are just as bright. Primary health care should not be delivered but encouraged.

[From ***Where There Is No Doctor: A Village Healthcare Handbook,*** **David Werner** and **Carol Thuman**]

Lay Health Advisors and Community Health Workers

Even where there are doctors and other professional resources, lay people can help advance community health. *From barbers to bartenders, farmers to shopkeepers, teachers to ministers, every community has its natural helpers – people seeking health or medical advice.*

Sometimes, these people may be more formally trained and utilized as community health workers. In China, they are *"barefoot doctors"*; in Hispanic/Latinx communities, they are called *"promotes."* While most of their work entails educating target audiences about health issues affecting their community, they also guide in accessing community resources associated with health care.

Community health workers are often residents and identified leaders in their community who work for community-based health promotion projects or as part of a research group. Thus, lay health advisors liaise with their community, health professionals, and human and social service organizations. *As liaisons, they often play the roles of advocate, educator, mentor, outreach worker, role model, and interpreter.*

Although they are not professional health workers, they are often tasked with projects similar to that of a professional health worker if the area where they work is significantly underserved (e.g., case management, referral source). Another highlight of the importance of lay health advisors is labor costs. *Even though they are not required and, in most instances, do not hold academic credentials (e.g., bachelor's or master's level degrees), they perform well enough, in general, to have similar improved outcomes to that of professional health workers but while working as volunteers or at a lower salary rate.*[177]

6.5: 10 Main Takeaways

1. Self-Care is Essential: Prioritizing self-care is vital for maintaining mental and physical health, helping you perform at your best, and fostering resilience.

2. Boosts Self-Esteem: Engaging in self-care practices enhances self-confidence and encourages a positive self-image, which is essential for navigating life's challenges.

3. Awareness of Personal Needs: Self-care fosters self-awareness, helping you effectively identify and fulfill your emotional and physical needs.

4. Creates Balance: Incorporating self-care routines into daily life promotes a balanced lifestyle, reducing stress and preventing burnout.

5. Improves Relationships: Nurturing yourself can cultivate healthier relationships, allowing you to support others better while maintaining your well-being.

6. Personalized Approach: A self-care plan should be tailored to your unique needs and evolve with your life changes to promote physical, mental, and emotional well-being.

7. Intentional Actions: Identify specific activities that nurture your health and happiness, whether through exercise, hobbies, or mindfulness, ensuring they are enjoyable and meaningful.

8. Build Habits Gradually: Start with small, manageable self-care activities and slowly incorporate more over time to create sustainable habits that fit your lifestyle.

9. Accountability and Flexibility: Use reminders to stay committed to your self-care routine while remaining flexible to adapt when life's challenges arise.

10. Reflect and Seek Support: Regularly assess your progress and share your goals with others for motivation, making self-care a collaborative and enjoyable journey toward improved well-being.

Book Summary

"By failing to prepare, you are preparing to fail."

— Benjamin Franklin

1.5: 10 Main Takeaways

1. Childhood Mischief: Embrace the lessons from my unconventional childhood experiences, emphasizing resilience and adaptability in facing challenges.

2. Value of Resilience: Resilience is essential for overcoming adversity. My childhood mischief taught me to persist despite the consequences.

3. Peer Influence: Understand how peer relationships can shape behavior and reinforce the importance of surrounding oneself with supportive friends.

4. Emotional Expression: Acknowledge the significance of emotional expression and vulnerability as pathways to personal growth and connection.

5. Cultural Expectations: Explore how cultural and familial expectations influence behavior, highlighting the courage needed to navigate these pressures.

6. Learning from Failures: Appreciate that failures are opportunities for learning and growth, helping to develop resilience and a strong sense of self.

7. Academic Excellence: While academic success is essential, resilience is crucial for long-term personal and professional fulfillment.

8. Ethical Foundation: Understanding ethics is crucial for making moral decisions. It emphasizes the importance of a shared moral code that guides individual and community behavior.

9. Moral Development: Recognizing the stages of moral development helps us appreciate how our sense of right and wrong evolves, shaped by experiences and societal influences.

10. Intergenerational Relationships: Fostering connections between generations enhances social cohesion and promotes mutual support, contributing to mental well-being and community resilience.

2.5: 10 Main Takeaways

1. Understanding Brain Responses: The brain reacts differently to "yes" and "no," with distinct regions involved in processing these words, impacting our behavior and emotions.

2. Neuroscience of Focus: Saying "no" enhances focus and decision-making, as emphasized by Steve Jobs' experiences in managing complexity.

3. Emotional Valence: "No" often carries a negative connotation, leading to slower responses and negative emotions, influencing how we interact socially.

4. Childhood Learning: Our sensitivity to "no" develops through caregiver interactions, shaping our emotional regulation and social behavior.

5. Neuroplasticity: The brain's ability to change (neuroplasticity) enables adults to grow new neurons, impacting memory, mood, and overall mental health.

6. Impact of Lifestyle: Engaging in healthy behaviors like learning and exercise can boost neurogenesis, promoting better mental health.

7. Stress Management: Saying "no" can reduce stress and enhance self-care, improving self-esteem and confidence.

8. Boundaries Matter: Establishing boundaries by saying "no" is essential for maintaining mental health and prioritizing personal needs.

9. Self-Esteem Development: Healthy self-esteem is crucial for motivation and decision-making, affecting overall quality of life.

10. Embrace Self-Acceptance: Recognizing and valuing oneself is critical to developing healthy relationships and achieving personal goals.

3.5: 10 Main Takeaways

1. The Sandwich Method: This technique frames negative feedback between positive remarks, making it easier to digest and fostering a supportive environment.

2. Constructive Criticism: Balancing praise and critique encourages openness, helping individuals feel valued while receiving necessary guidance.

3. Assertiveness Training: Develop skills to confidently express your needs and boundaries without feeling guilty or pressured.

4. Understanding No: Recognize that saying no is vital for personal well-being and can prevent burnout from over-commitment.

5. Role-Playing: Practice scenarios to become more comfortable saying no in various situations, enhancing your communication skills.

6. Easier Techniques: To make the process easier, implement straightforward strategies like smiling, standing, or preemptively saying no.

7. Cultural Awareness: Understand cultural differences in communication to navigate saying no in diverse environments effectively.

8. Authenticity Matters: Be genuine in your feedback to build trust and encourage growth.

9. Follow-Up Support: After delivering feedback, check in with others to show continued support and guidance.

10. Personal Growth: Embrace the journey of learning to say no to cultivate resilience and foster healthier relationships.

4.5: 10 Main Takeaways

1. Importance of Boundaries: Healthy relationships require boundaries, which are essential for maintaining emotional and mental well-being.

2. Avoiding Burnout: Establishing boundaries prevents burnout by protecting your energy and helping you manage personal demands.

3. Preventing Anger and Resentment: Clear boundaries can reduce the anger and resentment arising from overcommitting and neglecting one's needs.

4. Personal Identity: Boundaries help you maintain your individuality, allowing you to express preferences and needs without losing yourself in relationships.

5. Understanding Healthy vs. Unhealthy Boundaries: Recognizing differences is crucial; healthy boundaries enhance relationships, while unhealthy ones can lead to stress and conflict.

6. Strategies for Establishing Boundaries: Identify your needs, list essential boundaries, and communicate them effectively to those around you.

7. Empowerment: Setting boundaries is not selfish; it is a necessary act of self-care that empowers you to lead a fulfilling life.

8. Identifying Boundary Violations: Recognizing warning signs—like someone ignoring your "no" or demanding personal access—is vital for maintaining emotional safety.

9. Coping with Repeat Violations: Consistent boundary-setting is critical. Document violations and responses to identify weaknesses in your boundaries.

10. Choosing Healthy Relationships: Sometimes, you must decide whether to limit or cut contact with those who disrespect your boundaries, prioritizing your well-being over others' expectations.

5.5: 10 Main Takeaways

1. **Understanding Assertiveness**: Assertiveness involves expressing your opinions positively and confidently, balancing your needs with others.

2. **Assertiveness vs. Aggression**: Distinguish between assertive behavior, which respects others, and aggressive behavior, which prioritizes self-interest.

3. **Self-Value**: Recognizing your worth is essential for assertiveness. Understand that you deserve respect and should assert your rights.

4. **Confident Communication**: Voice your needs and goals to others without waiting for recognition.

5. **Control Your Reactions**: You can only control your behavior, not others. Stay calm and respectful, regardless of their responses.

6. **Positive Expression**: Constructively confront issues, express feelings, and maintain respect while being assertive.

7. **Acceptance of Feedback**: Embrace criticism and compliments positively to foster personal growth.

8. **Saying "No"**: Master "no" to protect your time and workload while seeking win-win solutions.

9. **Consistent Communication**: Use consistent words, tone, and body language to reinforce assertiveness.

10. **Continuous Improvement**: Regularly review your assertiveness progress to identify successes and areas for growth.

1. Self-Care is Essential: Prioritizing self-care is vital for maintaining mental and physical health, helping you perform at your best, and fostering resilience.

2. Boosts Self-Esteem: Engaging in self-care practices enhances self-confidence and encourages a positive self-image, which is essential for navigating life's challenges.

3. Awareness of Personal Needs: Self-care fosters self-awareness, helping you effectively identify and fulfill your emotional and physical needs.

4. Creates Balance: Incorporating self-care routines into daily life promotes a balanced lifestyle, reducing stress and preventing burnout.

5. Improves Relationships: Nurturing yourself can cultivate healthier relationships, allowing you to support others better while maintaining your well-being.

6. Personalized Approach: A self-care plan should be tailored to your unique needs and evolve with your life changes to promote physical, mental, and emotional well-being.

7. Intentional Actions: Identify specific activities that nurture your health and happiness, whether through exercise, hobbies, or mindfulness, ensuring they are enjoyable and meaningful.

8. Build Habits Gradually: Start with small, manageable self-care activities and slowly incorporate more over time to create sustainable habits that fit your lifestyle.

9. Accountability and Flexibility: Use reminders to stay committed to your self-care routine while remaining flexible to adapt when life's challenges arise.

10. Reflect and Seek Support: Regularly assess your progress and share your goals with others for motivation, making self-care a collaborative and enjoyable journey toward improved well-being.

Conclusion

"The difference between successful people and really successful people is that really successful people say no to almost everything."

— Warren Buffett

In conclusion, **"Dare to Embrace NO"** is more than just a guide to saying no—it's a powerful tool for personal transformation and mental well-being. By taking the courageous step to say no when necessary, you pave the way for a personal and professional life filled with resilience, confidence, and balance.

The journey begins with understanding the **foundations of resilience**. Reflecting on my **weird childhood** and the **emotional struggles** influenced by **peer pressure** and **cultural expectations**, you'll recognize that resilience is not just about enduring hardships but about making mindful choices. By setting clear boundaries early on, you can protect your mental health and nurture relationships that matter.

We are exploring **the neuroscience behind saying no, which** sheds light on how our brain functions when we assert ourselves. Understanding the roles of various **brain regions**, such as the **prefrontal cortex**, and the concept of **neuroplasticity** empowers you to rewire your mind, making it easier to establish **healthy boundaries**. This scientific insight is crucial in boosting your **self-esteem** and fostering a stronger sense of self-worth.

In the practical segment of the book, you'll find actionable strategies that can be immediately applied in your daily life. Techniques like the **Sandwich Method** and **Assertiveness Training** offer a structured approach to saying no while maintaining positive relationships. Including **Role-Playing Scenarios** allows you to practice these skills safely, making translating them into real-world situations easier. Overcoming **cultural and social barriers** is particularly important in the American context, where saying no can often feel uncomfortable or confrontational. This book provides you with the tools to navigate these challenges with confidence.

The final chapter, **The Power of Boundaries**, ties everything together by emphasizing the importance of protecting your time, energy, and mental health. Setting boundaries isn't selfish; it's about recognizing your worth and ensuring that your personal and professional life aligns with your values and goals.

For readers, the benefits of embracing no are immense. In a culture that often glorifies busyness and constant availability, learning to say no is a radical act of self-care. It allows you to reclaim time, reduce stress, and focus on what truly matters. This shift improves mental health and enhances productivity and job satisfaction. By prioritizing your well-being, you become more effective in your roles and more present in your relationships.

Essentially, **"Dare to Embrace NO"** invites you to take control of your life, break free from the pressures of saying yes, and cultivate a healthier, more fulfilling existence. By the end of this book, you'll have the confidence and skills to say no with grace and conviction, unlocking the door to a more balanced, mentally healthy, and empowered life.

With deepest gratitude,

Sekhar Kumar Dey

References

1. https://scriptmag.com/features/balls-of-steel-the-zig-zag-screenwriting-career-path

2. https://www.verywellmind.com/john-b-watson-biography-1878-1958-2795550

3. https://www.verywellmind.com/classical-conditioning-2794859

4. Rilling M. How the challenge of explaining learning influenced the origins and development of John B. Watson's behaviorism. *Am J Psychol.* 2000;113(2):275-301.

5. Staddon JE, Cerutti DT. Operant conditioning. *Annu Rev Psychol.* 2003;54:115-44. doi:10.1146/annurev.psych.54.101601.145124

6. https://www.verywellmind.com/operant-conditioning-a2-2794863

7. https://brenebrown.com/art/dare-to-lead-you-cant-get-to-courage-without-rumbling-with-vulnerability/

8. https://personalfindev.com/blog/10-remarkable-and-courageous-people-who-changed-the-world

9. https://www.perkins.org/the-frost-king-incident/

10. Folkman S, Moskowitz JT. *Coping: pitfalls and promise. Annu Rev Psychol.* 2004;55:745-74. [PubMed] [Reference list]

11. Venner M. [Adjustment, coping and defense mechanisms--deciding factors in the therapeutic

process]. Z Gesamte Inn Med. 1988 Jan 15;43(2):40-3. [PubMed] [Reference list]

12. Neurosci Biobehav Rev. 2017 Mar;74(Pt B):401-422. [PubMed] [Reference list]

13. Coppens CM, de Boer SF, Koolhaas JM. Coping styles and behavioral flexibility: towards underlying mechanisms. Philos Trans R Soc Lond B Biol Sci. 2010 Dec 27;365(1560):4021-8. [PMC free article] [PubMed] [Reference list]

14. Kato T. Frequently Used Coping Scales: A Meta-Analysis. Stress Health. 2015 Oct;31(4):315-23. [PubMed] [Reference list]

15. Folkman S, Moskowitz JT. Coping: pitfalls and promise. Annu Rev Psychol. 2004;55:745-74. [PubMed] [Reference list]:

16. Anxiety Stress Coping. 2011 Oct;24(5):477-97. [PubMed] [Reference list]

17. Folkman S, Moskowitz JT. Coping: pitfalls and promise. Annu Rev Psychol. 2004;55:745-74. [PubMed] [Reference list]

18. Psychol Bull. 2017 Sep;143(9):939-991. [PMC free article] [PubMed] [Reference list]

19. Coppens CM, de Boer SF, Koolhaas JM. Coping styles and behavioral flexibility: towards underlying mechanisms. Philos Trans R Soc Lond B Biol Sci. 2010 Dec 27;365(1560):4021-8. [PMC free article] [PubMed] [Reference list]

20. Koolhaas JM, de Boer SF, Coppens CM, Buwalda B. Neuroendocrinology of coping styles: towards understanding the biology of individual

variation. Front Neuroendocrinol. 2010 Jul;31(3):307-21. [PubMed] [Reference list]

21. https://organizations.headspace.com/blog/harnessing-the-power-of-storytelling-to-improve-your-mental-health#:~:text=In%20honor%20of%20Mental%20Health,people%20accurately%20perceive%20their%20experiences.

22. https://www.psychologytoday.com/us/basics/intuition

23. https://www.psychologytoday.com/us/blog/am-i-right/201202/are-infants-moral https://www.psychologytoday.com/us/blog/experiments-in-philosophy/200806/do-atheists-pose-threat-morality

24. https://www.psychologytoday.com/us/blog/animal-emotions/201001/are-nonhuman-animals-more-moral-human-animals-yes-they-are

25. https://www.psychologytoday.com/us/blog/hot-thought/201311/the-origins-morality

26. https://www.psychologytoday.com/us/articles/201309/when-virtue-becomes-vice

27. https://www.psychologytoday.com/us/blog/the-nature-deception/201910/some-lie-lot

28. https://www.psychologytoday.com/us/blog/cui-bono/201912/when-right-is-not-right

29. https://www.psychologytoday.com/us/basics/punishment

30. https://www.psychologytoday.com/us/basics/ethics-and-morality

31. https://doi.org/10.1332/policypress/9781861347213.003.0002

32. https://doi.org/10.46692/9781847427908.003

33. https://doi.org/10.1371/journal.pcbi.1004709

34. https://en.wikipedia.org/wiki/Intergenerationality

35. https://en.wikipedia.org/wiki/Social_identity_theory

36. Urick, Michael J.; Hollensbe, Elaine C.; Masterson, Suzanne S.; Lyons, Sean T. (2017-04-01). "Understanding and Managing Intergenerational Conflict: An Examination of Influences and Strategies". *Work, Aging and Retirement*. **3** (2): 166–185. doi:10.1093/workar/waw009. ISSN 2054-4642.

37. ." *www.simplypsychology.org*. Retrieved 2020-11-06.

38. https://archive.org/details/Kompendium17sprachig10102017Edition2017GenerationsIntergenerationalRelationshipsGenerationalPolicy

39. ." 8 May 2018. Retrieved 2020-11-06.

40. https://en.wikipedia.org/wiki/Intergenerationality

41. https://youtu.be/H8eP99neOVs

42. https://insight.openexo.com/the-power-of-saying-no-from-psychology-to-neuroscience/#:~:text=Alia%2DKlein%2C%20N,10.1037/1528%2D3542.7.3.649

43. https://insight.openexo.com/the-power-of-saying-no-from-psychology-to-neuroscience/#:~:text=O%E2%80%99Doherty%20J%2C%20Kringelbach%20ML%2C%20Rolls%20ET%2C%20Hornak%20J%2C%20Andrews%20C.%20Abstract%20reward%20and%20punishment

%20representations%20in%20the%20human%2
0orbitofrontal%20cortex.%20Nat%20Neurosci.%
202001%3B4(1)%3A95%E2%80%93102.

44. https://insight.openexo.com/the-power-of-saying-no-from-psychology-to-neuroscience/#:~:text=No%20means%20you%20are%20creating,priorities%20letting%20you%20feel%20powerless.

45. https://insight.openexo.com/the-power-of-saying-no-from-psychology-to-neuroscience/

46. https://www.healthline.com/health/rewiring-your-brain

47. https://youtu.be/B_tjKYvEziI

48. https://www.psychologytoday.com/us/basics/self-esteem

49. https://www.psychologytoday.com/us/basics/confidence

50. https://synergyhealthprograms.com/why-saying-no-is-important/#:~:text=The%20power%20of%20saying%20no,us%20to%20value%20ourselves%20more.

51. https://www.verywellmind.com/what-is-self-worth-6543764

52. Trzesniewski KH, Donnellan MB, Robins RW. Stability of self-esteem across the life span. *J Pers Soc Psychol*. 2003;84(1):205-220.

53. https://www.verywellmind.com/what-is-motivation-2795378

54. https://www.verywellmind.com/signs-you-may-be-a-perfectionist-3145233

55. von Soest T, Wagner J, Hansen T, Gerstorf D. Self-esteem across the second half of life: The role of socioeconomic status, physical health, social relationships, and personality factors. *Journal of Personality and Social Psychology*. 2018;114(6):945-958. doi:10.1037/pspp0000123

56. Johnson AJ. Examining associations between racism, internalized shame, and self-esteem among African Americans. *Cogent Psychology*. 2020;7(1):1757857. doi:10.1080/23311908.2020.1757857

57. https://www.verywellmind.com/what-is-unconditional-positive-regard-2796005

58. https://www.verywellmind.com/rumination-why-do-people-obsess-over-things-3144571

59. https://www.verywellmind.com/how-to-be-optimistic-4164832

60. https://www.verywellmind.com/say-no-to-people-making-demands-on-your-time-3145025

61. https://www.verywellmind.com/signs-of-low-self-esteem-5185978

62. Gabriel AS, Erickson RJ, Diefendorff JM, Krantz D. When does feeling in control benefit well-being? The boundary conditions of identity commitment and self-esteem. *Journal of Vocational Behavior*. 2020;119:103415. doi:10.1016/j.jvb.2020.103415

63. https://www.verywellmind.com/how-to-boost-your-self-confidence-4163098

64. Nguyen DT, Wright EP, Dedding C, Pham TT, Bunders J. Low self-esteem and its association with anxiety, depression, and suicidal ideation in Vietnamese secondary school students: A cross-sectional study. *Front Psychiatry*. 2019;10:698. doi:10.3389/fpsyt.2019.00698

65. https://www.verywellmind.com/what-is-narcissistic-personality-disorder-2795446

66. https://www.verywellmind.com/the-big-five-personality-dimensions-2795422

67. Brummelman E, Thomaes S, Sedikides C. Separating narcissism from self-esteem. *Curr Dir Psychol Sci*. 2016;25(1):8-13. doi:10.1177/0963721415619737

68. https://www.verywellmind.com/ask-a-therapist-how-can-i-improve-my-self-esteem-5095001

69. https://www.verywellmind.com/cognitive-distortions-and-stress-3144921

70. https://www.verywellmind.com/how-to-use-positive-self-talk-for-stress-relief-3144816

71. https://www.verywellmind.com/positive-affirmations-for-stress-relief-3144809

72. https://www.verywellmind.com/positive-affirmations-for-stress-relief-3144809

73. Cascio CN, O'Donnell MB, Tinney FJ, Lieberman MD, Taylor SE, Stretcher VJ, et. al. Self-affirmation activates brain systems associated with self-related processing and reward and is reinforced by future orientation. *Social Cognitive and Affective Neuroscience*. 2016;11(4):621-629. doi:10.1093/scan/nsv136

74. https://www.simplilearn.com/emotional-intelligence-what-why-and-how-article

75. https://synergyhealthprograms.com/mental-health-admission/

76. https://www.makingbusinessmatter.co.uk/attentive-listening/

77. https://www.makingbusinessmatter.co.uk/constructive-criticism/

78. https://www.harleytherapy.co.uk/counselling/saying-no.htm

79. https://www.impactfactory.com/resources/assertiveness-why-its-hard-to-learn-to-say-no/

80. https://www.healthyplace.com/depression/articles/assertiveness-non-assertiveness-and-assertive-techniques

81. https://www.impactfactory.com/resources/assertiveness-skills-the-art-of-saying-no/

82. https://www.indeed.com/career-advice/career-development/how-to-nicely-say-no

83. https://extension.psu.edu/cultural-differences-in-the-workplace

84. https://clockify.me/blog/business/focused-work-meeting/

85. https://clockify.me/work-life-quality-balance

86. https://www.washingtonpost.com/news/worldviews/wp/2017/04/24/how-close-is-too-close-depends-on-where-you-live/

87. https://hbr.org/2015/12/getting-to-si-ja-oui-hai-and-da

88. https://hbr.org/

89. https://clockify.me/blog/business/track-employee-performance/

90. https://www.shrm.org/topics-tools/news/hr-magazine/how-to-create-effective-cross-cultural-training-program

91. https://www.researchgate.net/publication/3251 73867 The impact of language barrier and communication style in organizational culture on expatriate's working performance

92. https://www.who.int/news/item/28-05-2019-burn-out-an-occupational-phenomenon-international-classification-of-diseases

93. https://onlinelibrary.wiley.com/doi/10.1002/9781118970843.ch333

94. https://fearlessliving.org/watch-out-for-these-5-signs-you-dont-trust-yourself/

95. https://fearlessliving.org/overcoming-self-doubt-why-youre-stuck-and-how-to-get-unstuck/

96. https://fearlessliving.org/how-taking-risks-can-lead-you-to-a-better-life/

97. https://fearlessliving.org/

98. https://www.whatsok.org/blog/how-will-i-know-when-my-boundaries-are-crossed

99. https://betterboundariesworkbook.com/types-of-boundaries/

100. https://fearlessliving.org/types-of-fear/

101. https://fearlessliving.org/why-personal-boundaries-are-important-and-how-to-develop-them/

102. https://www.mindtools.com/afjikkt/williams-12-strategies-for-controlling-aggression

103. https://www.sciencedirect.com/science/article/pii/S1877042810022317

104. https://www.columbia.edu/~da358/publications/ames_flynn_asscrtiveness.pdf

105.	https://pubmed.ncbi.nlm.nih.gov/8056571/

106.	Maxfield, D., Grenny, J., & McMillan, C. (2015). Gender Inequality: Women Judged More Harshly Than Men When Speaking Up Assertively [online].

107. https://www.mindtools.com/awe5sru/developing-self-awareness

108.	https://www.mindtools.com/an6w7cc/how-do-you-add-value-at-work

109.	https://www.mindtools.com/ap5omwt/how-to-build-self-confidence

110. https://www.mindtools.com/anenol6/managing-your-boundaries

111. https://www.mindtools.com/au6zora/humility

112. https://www.mindtools.com/a9bea9f/the-feedback-matrix

113. https://www.mindtools.com/av01nf5/how-to-avoid-generosity-burnout

114. https://www.mindtools.com/ajh8pyd/win-win-negotiation

115. https://www.mindtools.com/agz0gft/empathy-at-work

116. https://www.mindtools.com/a0iw9ix/formal-warnings

117. https://www.mindtools.com/amjhdie/assertiveness

118. https://www.artihalai.com/what-does-assertive-communication-coaching-offer-professionals/

119. https://www.artihalai.com/how-masterclasses-can-boost-your-professional-development-goals/

120. https://www.artihalai.com/tag/leadership-skills-development/

121. https://www.artihalai.com/tag/assertive-communication/

122. https://www.artihalai.com/how-to-build-confidence-for-public-speaking-according-to-a-seasoned-news-presenter/

123. https://www.artihalai.com/feedback-strategies-how-to-give-and-receive-constructive-feedback/

124. https://www.artihalai.com/tag/constructive-feedback/

125. https://www.artihalai.com/tag/effective-communication/

126. https://www.artihalai.com/effective-communication-and-conflict-resolution-a-step-by-step-guide/

127. https://www.artihalai.com/enhancing-communication-skills-via-emotional-intelligence/

128. https://www.artihalai.com/tag/personal-growth/

129. https://www.artihalai.com/overcoming-barriers-to-assertiveness-3-key-strategies/

130. https://qr.ae/p2tFuS

131. https://www.perimeterhealthcare.com/news/posts/the-importance-of-self-care

132. https://www.behappier.com/blogs/articles/why-is-self-care-important-how-does-it-help?srsltid=AfmBOorOSScrKQFgYkOt8o4Hyhdy8zELMYsMVFd6xZf6xPjfJBqWcI6k

133. https://today.marquette.edu/2024/08/the-importance-of-self-care-for-maintaining-mental-health/

134. https://www.perimeterhealthcare.com/news/posts/the-importance-of-self-care

135. https://www.forbes.com/health/mind/self-care-gifts/

136. https://www.choosingtherapy.com/emotional-self-care/

137. https://www.choosingtherapy.com/repressed-anger/

138. https://www.choosingtherapy.com/journaling-for-mental-health/

139. https://www.choosingtherapy.com/affirmations/

140. https://www.choosingtherapy.com/how-to-practice-gratitude/

141. https://www.choosingtherapy.com/financial-abuse/

142. https://www.choosingtherapy.com/meditation/

143. https://www.choosingtherapy.com/grounding-techniques/

144.   https://www.choosingtherapy.com/types-of-self-care/

145. https://www.calm.com/blog/how-to-focus-on-yourself?utm_medium=organic&utm_source=blog&utm_campaign=self-care-plan

146.   https://www.calm.com/blog/health-hacks?utm_medium=organic&utm_source=blog&utm_campaign=self-care-plan

147. https://www.calm.com/blog/how-to-love-yourself?utm_medium=organic&utm_source=blog&utm_campaign=self-care-plan

148.   https://www.calm.com/blog/5-simple-ways-to-practice-mindfulness-in-daily-life?utm_medium=organic&utm_source=blog&utm_campaign=self-care-plan

149.   https://www.calm.com/blog/how-to-be-happy-again?utm_medium=organic&utm_source=blog&utm_campaign=self-care-plan

150.   https://www.calm.com/blog/how-to-get-motivated?utm_medium=organic&utm_source=blog&utm_campaign=self-care-plan

151. https://www.calm.com/blog/what-to-do-when-you-feel-

overwhelmed?utm_medium=organic&utm_sourc
e=blog&utm_campaign=self-care-plan

152. https://www.calm.com/blog/mood-
monitoring?utm_medium=organic&utm_source=
blog&utm_campaign=self-care-plan

153. https://www.calm.com/blog/what-is-
mindfulness-
meditation?utm_medium=organic&utm_source=
blog&utm_campaign=self-care-plan

154. https://www.calm.com/blog/meditation-for-
beginners?utm_medium=organic&utm_source=b
log&utm_campaign=self-care-plan

155. https://www.calm.com/blog/healthiest-
lifestyle?utm_medium=organic&utm_source=blo
g&utm_campaign=self-care-plan

156. https://www.calm.com/blog/how-to-focus-on-
yourself?utm_medium=organic&utm_source=blo
g&utm_campaign=self-care-plan

157. https://www.calm.com/blog/yoga-for-
relaxation?utm_medium=organic&utm_source=b
log&utm_campaign=self-care-plan

158. https://www.calm.com/blog/personal-
goals?utm_medium=organic&utm_source=blog&
utm_campaign=self-care-plan

159. https://www.calm.com/blog/mindful-
eating?utm_medium=organic&utm_source=blog
&utm_campaign=self-care-plan

160. https://www.calm.com/blog/how-to-sleep-
better?utm_medium=organic&utm_source=blog
&utm_campaign=self-care-plan

161. https://www.calm.com/player/6oIdD95DvF?ut
m_medium=organic&utm_source=blog&utm_ca
mpaign=self-care-plan

162. https://www.calm.com/blog/how-to-
practice-self-
compassion?utm_medium=organic&utm_source
=blog&utm_campaign=self-care-plan

163. https://www.calm.com/blog/tips-for-
managing-
stress?utm_medium=organic&utm_source=blog
&utm_campaign=self-care-plan

164. https://www.calm.com/blog/how-to-stop-
worrying?utm_medium=organic&utm_source=bl
og&utm_campaign=self-care-plan

165. https://www.calm.com/app/program/euLMnJX
PGG?utm_medium=organic&utm_source=blog&
utm_campaign=self-care-plan

166. https://www.calm.com/blog/9-tips-for-
setting-healthy-
boundaries?utm_medium=organic&utm_source=
blog&utm_campaign=self-care-plan

167. https://www.calm.com/blog/how-to-start-
meditating-

daily?utm_medium=organic&utm_source=blog&utm_campaign=self-care-plan

168. https://www.calm.com/blog/outdoor-meditation?utm_medium=organic&utm_source=blog&utm_campaign=self-care-plan

169. https://www.calm.com/blog/mental-fitness?utm_medium=organic&utm_source=blog&utm_campaign=self-care-plan

170. https://www.calm.com/blog/professional-development-goals?utm_medium=organic&utm_source=blog&utm_campaign=self-care-plan

171. https://www.calm.com/blog/mental-health-goals?utm_medium=organic&utm_source=blog&utm_campaign=self-care-plan

172. https://www.calm.com/blog/mindfulness-exercises?utm_medium=organic&utm_source=blog&utm_campaign=self-care-plan

173. https://www.calm.com/blog/how-to-find-your-passion?utm_medium=organic&utm_source=blog&utm_campaign=self-care-plan

174. https://www.calm.com/blog/tips-for-managing-stress?utm_medium=organic&utm_source=blog&utm_campaign=self-care-plan

175. https://www.linkedin.com/pulse/breaking-down-barriers-self-care-jolawn-victor/

176. https://hesperian.org/

177. https://humanjourney.us/health/the-pursuit-of-health/who-provides-care/?gad_source=1

Disclaimer

This book is for educational purposes only. Readers acknowledge that the author does not render legal, financial, medical, or professional advice. The content of the book has been derived from various sources. Please consult a licensed professional advice before attempting any techniques outlined in this book.

By reading this document, the reader agrees that the author is under no circumstances responsible for any direct or indirect losses incurred due to the use of the information contained within it, including but not limited to errors, omissions, or inaccuracies. Adherence to all applicable laws and regulations, including international, federal, state, and local governing professional licensing, business practices, advertising, and all other jurisdictions, is the sole responsibility of the purchaser or reader.

Neither the author nor the publisher assumes any responsibility or liability on behalf of the purchaser or reader of these materials. Any perceived slight of any individual or organization is purely unintentional.

Your Voice Matters: May I ask you for a small favor?

Honored Readers,

First, I want to thank you for reading this book. You could have chosen any other book, but you took mine, and I appreciate this.

I hope this message finds you healthy and happy as you read these lines. I am incredibly grateful as I write this letter and reflect on the travels we have experienced together within the pages of my book, "Dare To Embrace No." Your everlasting faith in me and unfailing encouragement have given me valuable motivation and approval.

Your suggestions are essential to my creative process as an independent scribe. They fuel my passion and allow me to go deeply into the core of my creative attempts and find the heart of my writing. I respectfully ask that you consider posting a review for "Dare To Embrace No" to gain valuable insights and opinions.

Your review does not need to be in-depth or extensive; even a brief collection of ideas that expresses your true feelings will do. Whether your comments are compliments or constructive criticism, they are all essential building blocks in my search for ongoing development as a writer and storyteller.

Your review has more impact than words on a screen because it can influence potential customers and direct them on their literary journeys. Your advice essentially serves as a lighthouse, guiding me as I embark on new literary endeavors.

I implore you to set aside some of your valuable time to express your opinions in online journals or sites like Amazon, Goodreads, or whichever digital harbor serves as your entryway to my creative universe. By working together to ignite the spark of creativity in the hearts and brains of countless people, we can further strengthen our symbiotic relationship as readers and creators.

Please accept my sincere appreciation for your involvement in this literary journey. I am looking forward to the chance to share more stories that speak to the core of your minds and souls, and I am also looking forward to your upcoming reviews with great enthusiasm.

Keeping it straight – reviews are the lifeblood of any author.

Sincere regards,

(Sekhar Kumar Dey)